DOLLS' HOUSES
AND MINIATURES

VALERIE C. JACKSON

JOHN MURRAY · LONDON

This edition first published in Great Britain by
John Murray (Publishers) Ltd
50 Albemarle Street
London W1X 4BD

British Library Cataloguing in Publication Data

Jackson, Valerie
  Dolls' Houses and Miniatures
  I. Dolls' houses, 1700–1950
  I. Title
  688.7′23′0903

  ISBN 0–7195–4615–X

Produced by the Justin Knowles Publishing Group
9 Colleton Crescent, Exeter, EX2 4BY

Designer: Peter Wrigley

Typeset by Keyspools Ltd, Golborne, Lancashire

Printed and bound in Portugal
by Printer Portuguesa

FRONTISPIECE
The Hall of the Guilds in Titania's Palace,
a sixteen-roomed palace in miniature (see
pages 147–9) that fetched £135,000
($236,250) when it was sold by Christie's
in 1977.

TITLE PAGE
One of the four "rooms", made of printed
cards slotted together, that formed a
McLoughlin folding house (see page 116).

CONTENTS

Introduction   6

Beginnings   7

The 17th Century   11

The 18th Century   43

The 19th Century   81

The 20th Century   127

Bibliography   158

Index   159

Acknowledgements   160

INTRODUCTION

Dolls'-house collectors are in good company – princes and princesses, dukes and duchesses have all fallen under the spell of this absorbing hobby. The undoubted fascination of dolls' houses is hard to explain adequately. It cannot be entirely put down to the attraction of smallness, or to the desire to escape from the everyday world. Other justifications have been offered – an interest in architecture, a love of fine craftsmanship, and nostalgia for a lost childhood (or, to put it more unkindly, "infantile regressive sentimentality"). But for many of us who enjoy studying social history, dolls' houses are a three-dimensional reflection in miniature of the way we once lived, little theatres bringing domestic history to life, and we are grateful that so many have survived in museums, collections, and country houses to tell the the tale.

Whatever our reasons for appreciating them, dolls' houses have captured our imagination for over four centuries, encouraging grown men and women to spend hours, and sometimes fortunes, on the creation of these worlds in miniature, a pursuit which has continued well into modern times, when not even the lack of space or money can deter the dedicated enthusiast.

Shops are scoured for dolls'-house items; kitchens and basements are turned into workshops for the manufacture of fixtures and fittings; and small-scale copies of real-life houses are commissioned regardless of expense as we, like our ancestors, re-create households in miniature for the entertainment and enlightenment of future generations.

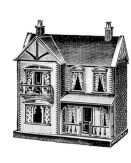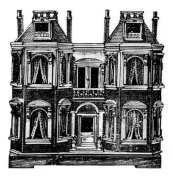

Three dolls' houses from the G. & J. Lines 1909–10 catalogue. In the centre, priced at 75s (£3.75, $18.25), is the Kits Coty house (see page 144), described as "a really splendid mansion, elaborately fitted up, inside and out. Staircase, doors to rooms. French windows. Curtains, beautiful papers on walls etc. 33 in high." Flanking it are more modest, balconied houses.

BEGINNINGS

There have been models of houses and everyday cooking utensils from the earliest times. Such models were not necessarily made for children. Many were funerary offerings, intended to serve the needs of the departed when they reached the next world. So we find ancient Egyptian bakeries and granaries peopled with model slaves to prepare food for their masters – the Egyptians were nothing if not practical. At the Metropolitan Museum of Art in New York are the Meket-Re tomb models of a bakery, a granary, carpenter's and weaver's shops, and a garden. The British Museum, London, has a model of a granary, dating from about 1800 BC, made of wood that the dry atmosphere of the Egyptian tomb has fortunately preserved. The model is 18 in (46 cm) by 24 in (60 cm) in plan. The granary has a hatch with sliding doors to receive the grain. In the courtyard a woman is grinding barley in front of a flight of stairs leading to a shelter on the granary roof where a watchman, or possibly the owner, sits in comfort.

That there were toys made especially for children is proved by more recent exhibits at the British Museum – terracotta toys, all of about 450 BC, from Melos, Crete, and Corinth, of a monkey riding a mule, seated girls, a monkey with a pestle and mortar, and a jointed dancing doll.

These objects possibly indicate the existence of small houses in which to place them. Like the young girls of Nuremberg centuries later, Athenian girls received their education at home, and there would be no better way to teach them their domestic duties than with a miniature house filled with everyday household items.

Not intended as dolls' houses, but demonstrating past interest in the world of the miniature are various models of houses in museums. There is a fine Etruscan model of a house dated 9–10 BC in the Tarquinia Museum, Italy. A Chinese Han-dynasty tomb building dated between about 200 BC and AD 220 is in the W. R. Nelson Gallery of Art in Kansas City. The British Museum has an earthenware funerary model from China of a house complex of about AD 15; it has a courtyard, a reception hall with lattice windows, a granary, a storehouse, and smaller side buildings representing living quarters and kitchens.

These tantalizing clues from ancient times are sparse enough but they seem generous compared with the void that exists from Roman times to about the 13th century. The Dark Ages have left behind few traces of children's playthings, but there may have been none to leave. Children, especially girls, were poorly considered. The times were hard and comfortless; plague and pestilence could, and did, wipe out whole populations. Belongings were burnt to prevent the spread of infection, which left little remaining in wood. Yet, in spite of this, as Karl Gröber notes in his book *Children's Toys of Bygone Days*, toy domestic utensils were found under the ruins of Osterburg Castle, which was destroyed in 1270, so playthings did exist.

By the 15th century, Europe was becoming more peaceful. Guilds were formed, giving craftsmen training and support and setting fair prices. But there was no early guild of toy makers. Many decades passed before craftsmen in any numbers turned to the manufacture of playthings. It seems to have begun in Germany. Nuremberg, placed as it was at a convenient distribution point, became an early centre of the toy industry. It had a strong tradition of art and craft and became famous in the 15th and 16th centuries for its goldsmiths, silversmiths, and other metalworkers.

Making miniatures instead of full-sized objects was a natural progression for these craftsmen, especially as at about this time, now that the rich could abandon their uncomfortable castles and live in unfortified houses, there arose the craze for forming collections.

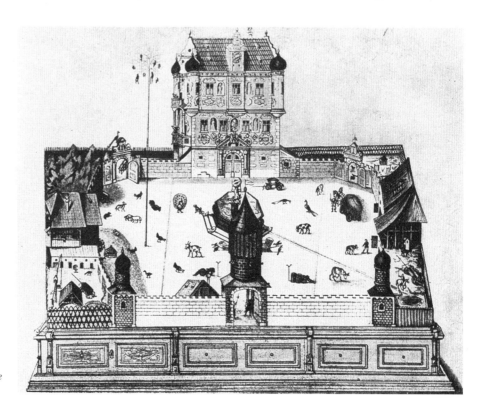

A drawing (c.1640) of a model house and courtyard, now lost, made in 1617 for Duke Philip of Pomerania (see page 24).

Cabinets were made to hold little works of art and curios, a collecting craze that stimulated the toy industry. Human nature has not changed much in 400 years, and giving silver toys to children justified the expense to parents, much as today a father may justify the expensive purchase of a toy train set by pretending that he is buying it for his son.

Silver toys were popular among the children of the very wealthy. In her book *Toys of Other Days* Mrs F. Nevill Jackson tells us that in 1576 "an order was given by the daughter of Henry II of France for a little silver toy set, composed of buffet pots, plates, bowls, and other vessels for the domestic menage, 'such as they make in Paris,' to be sent to the new-born child of the Duchess of Bavaria". Valuable toys are mentioned in the time of Henry IV of France (1553–1610). Later still, in 1607, Héroard, physician to the young Dauphin of France (later Louis XIII), recorded that the six-year-old Dauphin went to the Queen's chamber where he made a fire and cooked a stew in his own small cooking vessel.

It is just possible that Italy may have been the first country to produce a dolls' house, some historians believing that the strong tradition of the crèche, with its elaborate representations of the Nativity, may have been related to dolls'-house making. Many crèches contained a great deal of detail, such as miniature pots and models of real-life items, which must have delighted children (though they would not have been allowed to play with them) as well as adults. Unfortunately, though, for this tempting theory, there is no record of any Italian dolls' house in existence before the 18th century. Dolls' houses, in fact, seem to come primarily from northern Europe, where, perhaps because of the climate, life has always been centred on the home. They are less common in southern Europe, where the tradition of the crèche is strongest, and are found in greater numbers in Protestant countries sharing the same regional background as that of the early traditions of the Christmas tree, proliferating in countries where modern childcare first evolved.

It is not until the middle of the 16th century that the history of the dolls' house ceases to become conjectural. Then, in 1557 or 1558, Duke Albrecht of Bavaria (whose mother, Duchess Jakobea, may herself have owned a dolls' house) had a dolls' house made for his small daughter. It was a miniature replica of a house of a German prince, designed to show off his possessions and life style. Duke Albrecht did not, when it was finished, give it to his daughter; he put it in his museum. A detailed inventory of the house, made in 1598, tells us why: it was too good to be a child's plaything.

The building was large, four storeys high. On the lower floor there was a yard with a fountain, a garden with a silver well, a stable, a cow barn, a dairy, and other domestic offices. Above this was a bathroom (containing four dolls – the mistress and three daughters washing), a dressing room, a kitchen (in which a chef doll was cutting open a pike), a courtyard, and an orchard with wire-work trees and flowers. On the

9

next floor was a ballroom, a bedroom, and a withdrawing room and on the top was a chapel, another kitchen, nurseries, a sewing room, and a bedroom containing three beds. The house was inhabited by more dolls – royal personages, servants, and courtiers – and was sumptuously equipped with silver pieces, rich tapestries, and fabulous furniture.

Duke Albrecht was clearly consumed by dolls'-house fever. Ten years after this first venture he commissioned Jacob Sandtner to create scale models of his five official residences, all of which were displayed with the original dolls' house in his museum in Munich. Unhappily for us all the contents of the museum were lost when it was destroyed by fire in 1674, leaving us with no visual record of a dolls' house until 1611, which is the date of the earliest known example in existence.

THE 17TH CENTURY

Throughout the 17th century and indeed right up to the late 18th or early 19th century, dolls' houses were known as "baby houses", "baby" at that time being the usual name for doll. Baby houses were not considered as toys in our sense of the word; they were for the display of wealth as well as for the education of young women who would later have to run houses and who needed to know what, for example, a well-equipped kitchen would require and what each utensil was for.

The kitchen of the earliest known dolls' house in existence – a German house of 1611 (see page 12) – with a fine array of dishes, ladles, strainers, bowls, platters, jugs, and plates.

GERMAN DOLLS' HOUSES

The earliest German dolls' houses are simple representations of houses, heavy wooden cabinets divided into rooms, with a central staircase. Some have balustrading in the front and all are huge. The earliest known dolls' house in existence, a 1611 house in the Germanische Nationalmuseum in Nuremberg, is nearly 9 ft (2.75 m) high, 6 ft (1.8 m) wide, and 2 ft (0.6 m) deep. (One wonders, incidentally, how visitors viewed these houses in days past; a step-ladder arrangement may have been provided, but the dolls' houses must have been quite dark inside. Perhaps our bright photographic lights are enabling us to see the fine detail as it has rarely been seen before.) The base of the house, which contributes considerably to its height, is the cellar. It has several doors, inside two of which are paintings of a maid taking an undressed child to the bathroom and of a servant polishing riding boots.

The ground floor is occupied by the great hall, decorated with a painting copied from an etching by Jan Sadeler, showing a lively gathering of men and women seated around a table in a garden. Particularly charming touches are the rabbit and dog underneath the benches round the wall.

Next to the hall is a large yard with a triple gallery, at the back of one of which is a painting of priests and nuns in festive mood. Some

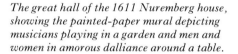

The great hall of the 1611 Nuremberg house, showing the painted-paper mural depicting musicians playing in a garden and men and women in amorous dalliance around a table.

garden plants grow up a trellis and, in the centre of the yard, a well is painted behind the flower bed. A staircase with another wall-painting leads to the first floor, where there is a kitchen filled with the utensils used at that time, most of them recognizable to anyone who has had experience of cooking. There is also a living room which was modernized in the 18th century.

On the second floor is a bedroom containing a huge bed and a state room with ornate 17th-century wooden furniture, including a fine linen press. Women took great pride in their linen, and a daughter would be given a good supply of it for her dowry, so presses in the German (and, as we shall see, Dutch) cabinets are full of bed and table linen and of uncut linen ready for making up later.

It was not only aristocrats and wealthy people who were interested in baby houses in Germany at this time. In 1631 an enterprising Nuremberg widow named Anna Koferlin had made a large house, 8 ft 6 in (2.6 m) high, which people paid to see. As she had sold most of her belongings to pay for the house, she doubtless needed the money. Although the house no longer exists, we get a very good idea of what it looked like from a woodcut on the cover of a booklet Anna Koferlin wrote as an advertisement. Childless herself, she claimed to have the educational interests of the young much at heart – the house was intended to be instructional, "so that when in time you have your own home and God willing your own hearth, you will for all your life put things nicely and properly, as they should be, in your own households...".

Even more domestic detail is seen in a 1639 house (also in the Germanische Nationalmuseum in Nuremberg), which is often referred to as the Stromer house, after its last owner, Baron von Stromer. At a little under 7 ft (2.1 m) high, it is slightly smaller than the 1611 house. It contains over a thousand small and very small objects, giving a unique picture of domestic life in a prosperous 17th-century German house.

This cabinet is divided differently from the earlier model, for the bottom storey has two sets of four workrooms on either side of the main entrance. On the left are horses and a cow in a byre, a wine store, a general store, and a servant's bedroom. On the other side is the nursery, with a cradle, a baby walker (a wooden frame that supported a young child learning to walk), and a cupboard bed for the nurse. There is also a maid's room with a baby in a cradle and, below, a shop with office and laundry. (Continental merchants of the 17th and 18th centuries incorporated their offices and counting houses in their homes, which enabled them to keep a sharp eye on their businesses while still taking a part in domestic life.) The six grander rooms are balustraded. On the first floor right is a lavishly equipped kitchen – kitchens had to be full of implements in an age when everything was prepared from raw materials. The deep fireplace, the focal point of the kitchen, has a chimney large enough to smoke ham and sausages, a spit, and a clockwork jack for roasting meat. Other items in the kitchen are

The kitchen of the Stromer house, with, on the wall beside the door, its memo board picturing the household wants list.

*The bedroom (described on page 17) of the
Stromer house, with its fine ceramic stove
by the bed and framed seascapes high on the
walls.*

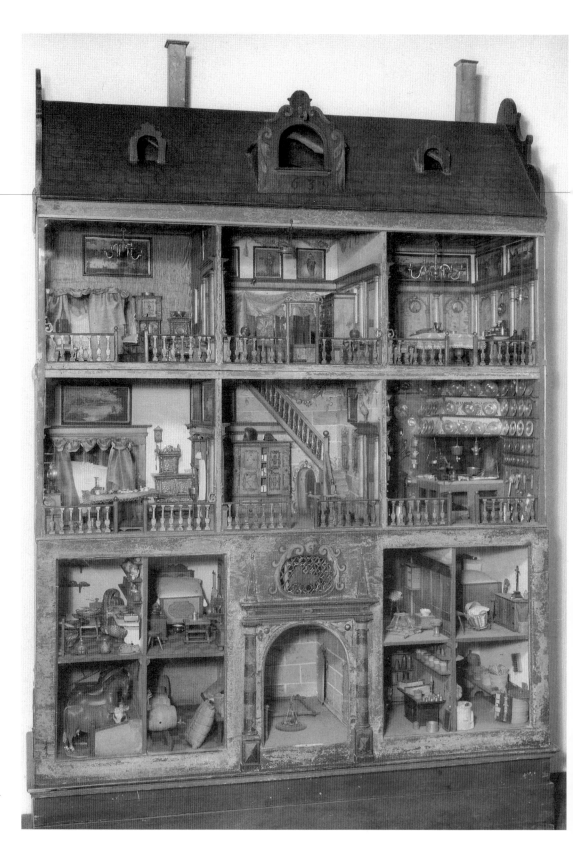

The distribution of rooms in the Stromer house. The balustrades of the upper rooms are not turned, they are painted on flat wood.

weights, the board on which household wants were depicted (not written – the servants would have been illiterate), graters, a chafing dish for cooking small dishes on charcoal, a copper pan with a tap on the bottom for hot water, pewter and brass plates, and a wooden meat safe with a painting of a girl on it.

Next to the kitchen is a hall. On the left is a bedroom with a curtained bed filled with feather cushions, a ceramic stove, fine paintings, a copper warming pan, a wash stand, and a close-stool.

On the top floor is another bedroom containing a stove and fine paintings, an upper landing, and a reception room.

A third important cabinet house at the Nationalmuseum in Nuremberg is the Kress house, dating from the second half of the 17th century, which also has a balustraded front. This house, unlike the two preceding ones, is inhabited by a family of dolls'-house dolls, but these

The huge earthenware stove, tapestry-covered chairs, and table laid with glass and silverware in the reception room of the Kress house. Note the fine row of plates above the panelling and the ornament and candlestick on the side table.

Like the Stromer house, the Kress house (RIGHT) has its living rooms over the service rooms. The crammed bottom floor holds a stable, with the ostler's room over, the servants' hall, with staircase to the upper floors, and a storeroom with a servant's room above it.

OPPOSITE : *another late-17th-century house, the Baumler house (see page 20), has a room arrangement very similar to that of the Kress house – even to the stable, occupied by two horses, on the left of the bottom level.*

are of the 18th century. On the bottom level are a servants' hall flanked by a stable, two servants' bedrooms, and storerooms. There are also four big family rooms, a kitchen, a panelled reception room, and two bedrooms, one of them a nursery occupied by a lady carrying a wax baby. Other occupants are a wax baby in a high chair, a lady in the upper hall, a lady sitting in the bedroom, a cook in the kitchen, a finely dressed man in the reception room and a maidservant in the servants' hall.

The fourth Nuremberg house of note is the Baumler house, dating from the last quarter of the 17th century. In *Toys of Other Days* Mrs F. Nevill Jackson gives a graphic and detailed description of this house.

There is ground floor, first and second. The hall is in the centre and has two pillars, and one sees a garden in the distance with a row of trees, a summer-house and a fountain; these are painted on the farther wall. A curious old lamp and bracket candlestick furnish the artificial light. On the right, a door leads into the shop or store-room where it was customary in the seventeenth century, when large houses were almost entirely self-contained, to buy, not only spices and every comestible, but also dress materials. A large blue cupboard with side compartment contains the stuffs carefully sorted in layers; in the drawers and on a narrow side table are pots, baskets, barrels, and hampers; sugar-loaves are on a shelf, and loaves brown and crisp-looking; a bunch of sponges hangs on the wall. A counter runs down the middle of the room on which weights and scales, a ball of twine, and a till are standing.

On the left of the hall is the stable where two toy chestnut horses stand feeding at their manger. The coachman, four inches high, is wheeling a barrow up to the food-bin; other stable accessories lie about; a stable lantern hangs from the ceiling. Through an open door one sees into the coachman's bedroom, in which a bed, a table, with tools and baskets, are placed.

A narrow flight of stairs, a facsimile of the staircases to be seen in the old Nuremberg houses to-day, leads from the hall to the first floor; the landing has in it a spinning-wheel, a broom, and a miniature mangle. To the right we pass through (or should do if we were a doll) a door to the drawing-room, which has in it a fine green-tiled stove; tiny ornaments of men and animals are set upon the cornice. In the centre of the room is a round oak table; two small console tables are on each side of a painted panel; the chairs, of which there are six, are square in shape, reminding one of the Jacobean shape in England; they are upholstered in red plush; on one a finely-dressed lady doll is seated; her work basket is standing near . . . ; flowers are arranged in vases and are also growing in pots in the windows. A fine pewter coffee-set is on a well-made stand, and a pewter bread-crock stands by.

Not only does the room contain all these useful and ornamental objects, but the decorations are perfect. The floor is of polished oak, the walls panelled in oak; a frieze rail or shelf supports tiny oriental vases; pictures and looking-glasses hang against the panelling; a daintily carved bracket in ivory holds ornaments and extra cups and saucers. A graceful glass chandelier is hung from the oak ceiling; the pendant crystal drops are most realistic. A clock stands on a side table and a miniature silver watch hangs on a nail on the wall.

Such is the detail of this wonderful house that even after reading this description it is still possible to point out other delights – the portraits in the reception room, the woven baskets and garden tools in the stables, the brass cooking pots in the kitchen, the baby's cradle in the upstairs room, and the birdcage hanging from the upper landing, to mention just a few.

The shop, or perhaps storeroom, in the Baumler house – stacked with everything the household could possibly need.

21

The two-roomed 17th-century cabinet house in Nuremberg consists simply of a kitchen with a panelled bed-sitting room above.

Another 17th-century Nuremberg house at the Nationalmuseum is a two-roomed cabinet containing a spacious kitchen with pewter, copper, brass, iron, and wooden utensils and, above, a sitting room with a bed in one corner.

Britain is fortunate in having in its possession at the Bethnal Green Museum of Childhood in London the only Nuremberg-type house outside Austria and Germany. Dated 1673, the house has a working

The Nuremberg-type house in the Bethnal Green Museum of Childhood has a fine display of pewter on the shelves and walls of both its working and its "best" kitchens.

kitchen with weights, moulds, and pans and a cooking area. There is a wooden cage on one wall to hold some hapless bird or beast until it was ready for the cooking pot. There is also a state kitchen next door. (Houses of this period often had a "best" kitchen in which good pots and pans and china could be shown off.) Rather surprisingly, the two closets are situated behind the state kitchen – although it seems that in fact the back of a kitchen or under the stairs were quite usual places for the "conveniences". Above the kitchens is the bedroom, almost completely filled by the bed, occupied by a child in a baby walker. Next door is a sitting room containing a smaller bed and a large green stove.

Of this house, Mrs Jackson observes: "The artisan's house, which is dated 1673, measures 36 in by 36 in and is 18 in deep. It is divided into four rooms only, and has no entrance-hall or landings; the staircase is placed against the kitchen wall. The seven windows are latticed, thin sheets of talc being carefully divided with leaded squares. There are also three open attic windows; the centre one resembles the door of a warehouse – this curious survival of the combination of dwelling-house and warehouse having been left in the domestic architecture both of the Netherlands and Holland."

Other 17th-century Nuremberg-type houses can be seen in the Musée de l'Oeuvre de Notre Dame, Strasbourg; the Bayerische Nationalmuseum, Munich; the Museum Angewandte Kunste, Vienna; and the Historische Museum, Basel. This last house is 6 ft (1.8 m) high and has three rooms built into a cupboard. On the top floor is a panelled room almost filled with a huge cupboard with barley-sugar-twist columns, the pediment ornamented with angels' heads. In the corner is a stove and an attractive frieze runs around the top of the room. The centre floor is occupied by a kitchen with an efficient-looking 18th-century stove with shelves. The bottom floor is a storeroom, its barrels safely enclosed within a stout fence.

Some 17th-century German houses have been lost to us. One, of the early 17th century, was in the Berlin Castle Museum before World War II; all that remains of it today is a black-and-white photograph in the 1932 book *Children's Toys of Yesterday* by C. G. Holme. It has two sparsely furnished basement rooms with arched bottle-glass windows, a first floor containing two kitchens, a nursery, and another room too dark to see (though it might be a living room), and, on the top floor, a bedroom, dining room, and reception room.

Another lost early-17th-century house is a cabinet that was at the University of Uppsala. It was made by artist Philip Hainhofer, and said to have been bought by the town of Uppsala for presentation to King Gustavus Adolphus II of Sweden. It was full of mechanical toys and other realistic detail. Another model – it was not a house – was made by the same artist, in 1617, for Duke Philip of Pomerania. It was a courtyard, full of animals, with elaborate buildings. A drawing dated around 1640 (see page 8) gives us an idea of what it looked like.

Still very much in existence and of great interest in the context of

The three-roomed 17th-century cabinet house in the Historische Museum, Basel.

Nuremberg cabinet houses is the controversial West Dean house, which, were it authentic and were its self-proclaimed date of 1668 correct, would have been the oldest dolls' house in Britain. West Dean College in southern England was once the home of Edward James, patron of the arts and godson of King Edward VII.

This painted pine cabinet, 9 ft 8 in (3 m) high, is a plain, dark green cupboard with a gabled roof and glass fronts which reveal eight furnished rooms and four landings with stairs. It is probably a 19th-century structure whose compartments have been furnished, for there is a great mixture of pieces of various dates and of varying scale – tiny people in the farmyard placed alongside a giant cockerel in a cage, for example, and a huge wheelbarrow in one of the storerooms. The cabinet is crudely made, its floor roughly stained to represent tiles or wooden marquetry.

The bottom storey holds a stable and poultry yard complete with chickens; stairs lead up to two storerooms, above which are a kitchen and a dining room. The top floor has a panelled linen room and a panelled bedroom. There are many later items among the furnishings. In the kitchen, for instance, is an 18th-century Delft soup tureen and in the linen room a 19th-century hanging metal birdcage. A wooden

The West Dean baby house (OPPOSITE) *is dated 1668 on the dormer in the roof, but it is in fact much later. Some of the many interesting items in the kitchen* (RIGHT) *are later still.*

clothes chest contains two waistcoat fronts dated about 1760 and part of a 19th-century costume. There is a basket made of rolled paperwork – an 18th-century craft – in the second storeroom.

However, other items such as the wooden cupboard in the stable, the linen press containing linen, the wooden and metal kitchen utensils, and the tiny wax child in its metal walking frame all have a powerful feeling of authenticity. The painting on the door of the bath house of a barefoot maid carrying a baby is very reminiscent in style of a cellar-door painting in the 1611 Nuremberg house illustrated in Leoni von Wilckens' book *The Doll's House*.

The West Dean house is a mysterious one, leaving us with unanswered questions. Was it Edward James' mother, Evelyn, who collected the furniture and ordered the construction of the cupboard? Evelyn James (*née* Forbes) had married Edward's father in 1889 and they had travelled extensively. Did Mrs James design it? In England at that time very few people would have known what a Nuremberg house looked like.

Yet another partial 17th-century German house is to be found in Denver, Colorado, in the Rosenberg collection. Dr Rosenberg pur-

This detail of the kitchen in the West Dean house shows a household wants board reminiscent of that in the Stromer house (page 14). There is also a fine selection of kitchen utensils – pie dishes, a salt container, tubs, a dustpan and brush, scales, a rolling pin, a griddle, and a bread crock.

chased it while travelling in Europe in the days when it was still possible to find antiques as rare as this. Made in the style of the period and housed in the upper section of a 17th-century cabinet whose lower section with drawers was in too poor a condition to keep, it contains five rooms, the largest of them boasting a large curved staircase, which Dr Rosenberg had installed. The furnishings include a brass chandelier like the one in the two-roomed 17th-century house in the Nationalmuseum, Nuremberg.

DUTCH CABINET HOUSES

Splendid though the early German houses are, they pale beside the magnificence of the Dutch houses. Dutch houses were not intended as playthings or even as educational toys; their contents were too costly for that. Rather, they were the hobby of wealthy ladies with time on their hands who wished to represent in miniature the houses of their time. They were for display and to satisfy a passion for collecting.

The second half of the 17th century was a glorious period in Netherlands history. Having escaped from the the clutches of Spain, the Netherlands became one of Europe's greatest commercial powers. Its middle classes prospered. Its merchants dealt with cargo ships which sailed into their ports laden with spices from the Indies, wines from Madeira and France, glass from Venice, and porcelain from China. The Dutch dolls' houses celebrate this richness of material things and their owners' unashamed enjoyment of them.

The Petronella de la Court baby house in the Centraal Museum at Utrecht is such a house, showing us in precise detail how families filled their homes with precious works of art and collectors' treasures.

In the de la Court house dolls add life to the rooms and some human activity seems to be taking place in each one. A large nurse holds a child in leading reins on the first floor; a mother entertains a visitor in the lying-in room, while the wet nurse waits to feed the new baby. (The lying-in room is a feature of all Dutch dolls' houses and presumably was also a feature of real-life houses, in an age when married women spent much of their time producing children, not all of whom reached maturity.) A fashionably dressed gathering is being entertained in the painted music room, where a game of cards is being played for money, as the gold coins spilling out of a tiny purse testify.

The garden is a miracle of carefully observed detail, from the games of ivory skittles and draughts in the gazebo to the bead-and-wire plants on their cordons on the wall. You can even recognize the sunflowers, lemons, and roses. More detail abounds in the nursery, where there are small ivory toys on the table (a chair, a top, and a dog's bone), a half-finished piece of bobbin lace on a lace pillow, a birdcage, and a hanging comb holder on the wall beside the elaborately trimmed fireplace. Next door in the storeroom a maid is walking towards a well-filled egg rack, carefully avoiding the mouse trap on the floor. Wooden slats at the back of the room conceal her sleeping quarters (humble

Every room of the de la Court baby house (ABOVE) *is filled with precious works of art and collectors' treasures.*

OPPOSITE: *the Oortman house, another priceless 17th-century cabinet house (see page 33), impresses by the austere grandeur of its peopled rooms.*

compared with the nursery) and the main bedroom with its silk carpet and painted ceiling. The ceilings are remarkable throughout for their variety and beauty.

Food is being prepared in the kitchen. A barrel of mussels stands in the foreground and a cheese, a half-cut fish, and some muffins are dotted about the room. The silver fireplace is furnished with fire implements and coals are ready in a basket nearby. Though many of the kitchen utensils are of silver, small slipware bowls and jugs form a line along the top of the cupboard.

Delicately carved ivory pictures in the lying-in room and the men's room, carved ivory figures representing the four seasons in the garden, a silver filigree firegrate in the kitchen, and lace-edged tablecloths and a silver iron in the laundry room add touches of luxury to the surroundings.

The reception room (RIGHT) *of the Oortman house, with wall paintings by Nicolaas Piermont, and the best kitchen* (BELOW).

Laundry rooms are a prominent feature of Dutch baby houses and in this one three maids are working. Wash day was an important domestic occasion, taking place about four times a year, hence the need for a large supply of linen. Laundresses were engaged for a daily wage and their food, and the soaking, wringing, rubbing, boiling, rinsing, and starching must have left them exhausted. Even then, there would still have been plenty of work for the maids to complete at the end of the day.

The master of the house sits in his counting house among bundles of papers tied with ribbon, rolls of tobacco, books, bottles, and ledgers. When he needs a rest from his labours, there is a couch in the room at the back. Later he may join his friends for a pipe of tobacco and some masculine talk in the men's room next door, with its amber and ivory pictures and large oil paintings of nude women. A revolving globe in the corner will enable him to follow the progress of his profitable fleet.

The Petronella Oortman house in the Rijksmuseum, Amsterdam, also dated to the last quarter of the 17th century, is another priceless period cabinet. By coincidence, the museum possesses a painting of the dolls' house by Jacob Appel, showing the tortoiseshell veneer cabinet inlaid with pewter more or less as it is now but peopled with little figures as it once was. From the painting we can see that the hall has been altered. Previously showing a landscape, it now has grisaille (grey-and-white painting) decorations, but the reception room still has its wall paintings of Arcadian landscapes by Nicolaas Piemont. The flower painting in the fireplace tells us that it is summer (the hearth furniture is stored away in the loft). On the chimney breast is another painting, of birds in a park, and the folding rosewood table shows a parrot resting in a wreath of flowers. The lying-in room in the middle floor has a bed in an alcove and there is a linen cupboard on the right with piles of linen in it. The Rijksmuseum has a Pieter de Hooch painting, *At the linen closet*, which shows a housewife handing out linen from just such a cupboard, and the museum also possesses a full-sized silver kettle and an urn with a tap in it by Amsterdam silversmith Christiaan Waarenburg, just like the one in the dolls' house, as well as silver sconces, candlesticks, dishes, bells, oyster plates, and tobacco jars, which are also to be seen in miniature in the baby houses.

On the top floor is a nursery, with covered baby baskets, whitewashed walls, decorated windows, and two pictures. The linen room on the same floor has a peat loft where foot warmers and a rat trap are stowed, together with the hearth furnishings for the summer. Little knitted stockings hang from a rack over the ironing maid. In the tapestry room is a black-and-gold lacquered cabinet holding a shell collection, standing against walls covered in zigzag Florentine tapestry stitch. The best kitchen has a painted cupboard filled with good china and glass and a marble fireplace, while the working kitchen in the centre of the house has a small fireplace, a sink with taps, another cupboard full of blue-and-white china, and a trap door to the cellar below.

Quite a lot is known about the other late-17th-century baby house in the Rijksmuseum, the Margaretha de Ruyter house, which is now known as the Dunois house. Margaretha de Ruyter married a clergyman named Bernardus Somer in 1673, and there is a pincushion in the house with the date 1676 marked out in pins, the year that Margaretha's father died. However, it seems that the house was bought by Petronella Dunois as a dowry on her marriage to Peter van Groenendijk in 1677, so the date on the pincushion is possibly the date of the furnishing of the cabinet by Petronella.

The cabinet is occupied by several wax dolls, whose modelling is so good that they must have been made by an artist. There is a marked contrast, for instance, between the round, coarse face of the nurse and the refined features of the lady of the house, as well as a distinction in their clothes. The lady wears her hair dressed with ribbons in fan shape with two long ringlets falling in front. Her long silk overdress opens to show off the gold lace on the underdress. There are tiny bows everywhere, a double row on the lower sleeves and also on the men's and childrens' clothes. The cook wears a plain dress with its sleeves rolled back and a sacking apron.

Whoever furnished the house did so with great care. The storeroom next to the well-equipped kitchen contains all a storeroom should have – barrels of wine or beer secure behind wooden palings, dried fish

The well-furnished Petronella Dubois house has a storeroom, a kitchen, and a men's withdrawing room on the bottom level, a bedroom and reception room on the middle level, and another storeroom, a laundry, and a nursery on the top level.

hanging from a rail on the wall, jars of pickles, even a hog's head on a plate. The kitchen is fairly simple, with its large fireplace, rush matting, and toilet in the corner cupboard. There, too, are the foot warmers, indispensable items in most Dutch baby houses. (They were wooden boxes with pierced tops, often carved in intricate patterns, inside which were placed earthenware containers for charcoal. Apparently, when ladies went visiting or to church, their maids followed carrying footwarmers for their mistresses. They must have been a welcome comfort in the cold northern winters.)

The men's room is next to the kitchen, and here we find two occupants, one with a long pipe, the other holding a kite. The middle level contains a cheerful bedroom with fabric-covered walls and matching bed hangings and a reception room with marquetry floor, painted ceiling, and wooden fireplace. A linen cupboard holds neatly folded linen. On the top level are a laundry, a storeroom, and a nursery. The house has a great many silver objects. Even everyday items such as buckets, washtubs, tableware, spits, and a spray for cleaning the windows are made of silver.

When you see all the silver in these 17th- and 18th-century houses, you can understand that it takes a museum curator a day just to clean one house. A proper spring-clean can take weeks.

Dolls' houses from the 17th century are not so well represented in the rest of Europe. In his book *Jouets de France* (1920), Leo Clarétie describes in detail an Alsatian dolls' house of 1680 belonging to a Strasbourg family living in Paris. It was a large affair contained in a chest measuring 6 ft 6 in (2 m) long by 3 ft (0.9 m) high, but no trace of it remains today. However, there is a late 17th-century manor house in the Nordiska Museet, Stockholm, Sweden, inside which are a first-floor storeroom, a centre-floor kitchen with a low cooking range and small fire holes, and a top-floor hall with painted friezes. Few of the original

*The late-17th-century manor house in the Nordiska Museet, Stockholm, shown here both closed (*BELOW*) and open (*BOTTOM RIGHT*), has an impressive kitchen (*BOTTOM LEFT*).*

furnishings have survived. This plain-looking manor house came from Sodra Lindved castle, Scania (not Norra Lindved as was first thought), and is extremely interesting in that it looks like a real house, which is unusual at this early date. Flora Gill Jacobs, in her book *A History of Dolls' Houses*, quotes the description of a former curator: "The shape of the roof is typical for the Swedish manor house from the baroque. The first floor is a sort of store room, in the centre floor is the kitchen with lining of imitated glaze tile and the top floor contains a big hall with painted friezes around the walls above and down in the lower part but the tapestries between the friezes are lost."

AN ENGLISH DOLLS' HOUSE

Firmly in the cabinet-house idiom is a famous English dolls' house which once belonged to Ann Sharp, god-daughter of Princess (later Queen) Anne. This is the oldest English dolls' house known (though not the earliest dolls' house in England – the Nuremberg house at the Bethnal Green Museum predates it). It is inhabited by a delightful family of dolls.

Less formal and less splendid than the German and Dutch cabinets, this house was a child's plaything rather than a costly toy for an adult, which is one of the reasons why it is so charming. The history of the house is well documented, for it has been in the same family since it was made for Ann, daughter of John Sharp, Archbishop of York, probably not long after her birth in 1691. The house has been preserved, more or less as Ann left it, by the Bulwer Long family of Norfolk, with the names of the dolls written in a neat hand on slips of paper pinned to their dresses or coats. The complete household is presented to us in wax or wood, some modelled only to the waist, some with cardboard hands and arms. The baby and the daughter of the house are in the nursery upstairs with "Sarah Gill, ye child's maid". (The neat writing and the fact that the apostrophe is in the right place leads us to think that Ann had some help with the labelling from an older brother or sister.) Sarah Gill is prettily dressed, indicating the importance of her position in the house. "Fanny Long, ye chambermaid" is in the bedroom and in the boudoir stands "William Rochett, ye heir". "Roger, ye butler", dressed in blue livery, stands by the hall table. The unidentified lady coming down the stairs must be Lady Rochett, hurrying to meet the guests gathering in the reception room – "Lady Jemima Johnson", "Mrs Lemon", another unidentified lady, and Lord Rochett. Lady Jemima's husband, Sir William Johnson, is missing. On the bottom level we have the homely figure of "Mrs Hannah, ye house-keeper" and, in the servants' hall, a footman.

The house, measuring 5 ft 9 in (1.75 m) high and 5 ft 7 in (1.7 m) wide, is quite roughly constructed, which is strange considering that it was a gift from a future Queen of England to her godchild, but doubtless there were many demands on Anne's purse.

Ann Sharp's house is full of fascinating things, some of which were old when Ann played with her house – a top shelf above the rooms displays an embroidered glove which probably dates back to the time of James I. A little model of a man in a tricorn hat, sitting on some rocks, perhaps reflects the contemporary interest in exploration – John Tradescant, plant collector and gardener to Charles I, had died not long before, in 1663. There is also a spinning wheel, a model theatre, a tiny coach and horses, miniature china, and paper cut-out fashion figures.

In the nursery is a walnut cradle containing a wax baby in swaddling clothes, a large baby basket, a four-legged walnut stool holding a silver saucepan for warming the baby's food, a pair of turned ivory candlesticks, and a lignum-vitae and ivory kettle on a stand. (Lignum vitae is a hard, heavy wood, much used in 18th-century baby houses and these items are the forerunners of many such to be seen later.) Another unusual item in the nursery is a paper dolls' house with paper furniture. The boudoir is a curious place, dominated by an unprepossessing wax-relief portrait of Mother Shipton, a 15th-century English witch. How this portrait came to be in the boudoir is something of a mystery. Strange, too, are the delicately carved wooden chandelier which has somehow been placed inside a glass sphere and a pet monkey

The nursery of the oldest known English dolls' house, the Ann Sharp house.

wearing a flat hat and sitting on a chair. No wonder William Rochett, "ye heir", looks stunned by it all.

Ivory boxes containing little brushes and an ivory mirror are in the four-poster bedroom and the drawing room, decorated with patterned gold wallpaper, has a portrait of Queen Anne painted on the back of a playing card. A rough, wallpapered door leads to the hall, which also serves as the dining room and has an opening into a recess or upper cellar. Tradition has it that the gentlemen used to retire there after dinner to finish their wine.

Ann Sharp's house is a cabinet of nine furnished and doll-populated rooms with a shelf for miniatures above.

The hall is filled with lignum-vitae and ivory pieces such as a cruet (the largest bottle was known as the Bishop, followed in diminishing sizes by the Dean, Rector, and Curates), a cutlery box, and a wine cooler. A red lacquered corner cupboard, a table laid with Leeds creamware of a later date, a dish of pottery oysters, Charles II silver candlesticks, and a solitary silver tankard are also in the hall.

In the kitchen next to the hall there are massive bellows, a plate warmer, correctly scaled cooking utensils, and, at the old grate, a pig roasting on a spit. A store room beneath the kitchen contains a rocking

The hall of the house serves also as a dining room. Roger the butler, looking, it has to be said, rather slovenly, is waiting to serve at table.

Kitchenware (TOP) *from the Ann Sharp house – a copper saucepan, a silver colander, a brass pestle and mortar, and a silver grater.*

On a shelf at the top of the house are miniatures some of which may be older than the house itself – (ABOVE) *a coach with horses, a model theatre of painted and gilded wood, and a model house.*

horse and another odd-looking horse of ruched linen. The servants' hall is economically furnished with chairs and a table on which are some little lignum-vitae objects and a pack of playing cards. The housekeeper's room is better equipped; it has a chest of drawers, a chair, a dainty white-draped four poster, a mirror on a low chest, and two tin candlesticks.

MINIATURES

It is difficult for a collector today to acquire 17th-century miniatures. Most of those that have survived the years are all firmly wedded to their houses – which is of course the best place for them.

Mrs F. Nevill Jackson writes: "in the seventeenth century silver toys were in very general use amongst the children of the wealthy. Whole services were ordered for special occasions; complete house furnishings were made as well as single pieces, which were sold separately. Not only was the furniture of the *salon*, the toilet, the nursery and the kitchen reproduced, but horses, carriages, chariots, cabriolets, sledges, and trucks in miniature, though not always as children's toys but simply as trinkets and cabinet specimens. Men and women daintily carved in silver were also made that the games of the children should want nothing in their realism."

A large proportion of the silver toys were made in Holland, but special orders were carried out in Paris, London, Frankfurt, and other centres of the silversmiths' craft, a trend which continued into the 18th century. The pots, tankards, mugs, cups, basins, and platters that appeared were made also in pewter, though the pewter pieces are rarer today than the silver, probably because, being cheaper, they were treated less carefully. Nonetheless, complete sets of pewter articles are to be found in the Nuremberg houses.

Like their European cousins, the English royal family were dedicated collectors. The artistic Princess Mary, who later shared the throne of England with her husband, William of Orange, while living in Holland before her accession, ran up in 1683 a bill with her silversmith Adam Loofs for £400 for "silver playthings". The Bethnal Green Museum of Childhood in London has some fine 17th-century silver miniatures – including a silver tankard dated 1600–85 – and we can at least speculate that these originated in the royal collection.

There are some early pieces of silver in the Ann Sharp house, notably some silver snuffers on a tray, which bear the date mark 1686, but some of the furniture is of later date and it is difficult to say precisely what was made when. Here, too, are several objects made of lignum vitae, a substance which remained popular into the 18th century.

The pieces from the West Dean baby house also vary in date, but the utensils shown on page 42 may well be 17th-century, as may the baby in its walking frame. This house has a charming little "household wants" board, like those in German 17th-century baby houses, on which is painted a pictorial shopping list showing rabbits, duck,

A group of English and Dutch silver toys (LEFT) *from the Bethnal Green Museum. The candlesticks are only $1\frac{1}{2}$ in (3.8 cm) high, from which the scale of the rest of the items – including scent bottles, candle snuffers, and vinaigrettes – can be gauged. Accessories from the West Dean house are* (BELOW LEFT) *a tin lantern, a portable metal room heater, and a ceramic stove.*

vegetables, and other items needed for the table. Another interesting item at West Dean is the portable heater, in which, presumably, charcoal or coal was placed and which could be carried wherever needed. This resembles the apparatus standing by the fireplace in the 1611 house in Nuremberg, where you can also see a great many kitchen utensils, such as pewter plates, pottery bowls, ladles, and sieves.

The cream of 17th-century miniatures is to be found in the Dutch houses. The Petronella Oortman house at the Rijksmuseum, Amsterdam, contains furniture of rosewood, ivory, and silver by the silversmith Christiaan Waarenburg. There is a lovely black-lacquered shell

A carved wooden chair and a very small wax baby in a baby walker (ABOVE) *from the West Dean house and* (ABOVE RIGHT) *a detail of the bathroom. The painting on the door of a maid carrying a baby is reminiscent of the cellar-door painting in the 1611 Nuremberg house (see page 12).*

cabinet and other pleasing domestic details include, in the kitchen, a tiny birdcage and, in the reception room, a rosewood fold-down table decorated with a parrot inside a wreath of roses. The Petronella Dunois house, also in Amsterdam, has a small oval table supported by gilded putti and many delightful silver models of everyday articles, including a ewer and basin. The de la Court house at Utrecht has a wealth of carved ivory, including chairs with barley-sugar-twist legs, some fine drinking glasses, pieces of Chinese porcelain, and miniature paintings by well-known Dutch artists of the period.

THE 18TH CENTURY

A knowledge of 17th-century dolls' houses and their contents is a useful background for a collector, even though the likelihood of finding a house or miniature of this period is fairly remote for most of us. The 18th century is another matter, for it is still possible, by a stroke of good fortune, to find such things at an auction or in a dealer's shop, albeit in need of restoration and costing a small ransom. Some memorable baby houses were made in the 18th century.

GERMAN DOLLS' HOUSES

In Germany, there was a break-away from the cabinet-style house when the Duchess Augusta Dorothea of Schwartzburg-Gotha (1666–1751) devoted her widowhood to the creation of not so much a dolls' house, more a fully populated doll town. Still in existence, Mon Plaisir (page 47), as the duchess called it, consists of glass-fronted boxes of many kinds and sizes – Karl Gröber, in *Children's Toys of Bygone Days*, lists 26 houses, 84 rooms, and 411 dolls. To see them, the visitor walks through a series of enormous, high-ceilinged rooms lined with tiers of these "picture books", many of which, if not all, have been renovated at least once. The whole life of an 18th-century German town is portrayed in these boxes rather like a theatrical event, with realistic-looking dolls acting the parts of royal personages and citizens. To realize her dream and produce this amazingly detailed miniature world, the Duchess (later Princess) Dorothea went deeply into debt to pay for the materials and craftworkers. Every girl in the neighbourhood who could sew was pressed into service; two monks from Erfurt made the wax heads and hands of the models and an army of metal workers, cabinet makers, artists, and craftsmen was employed.

Daily court life in the princely residence of Mon Plaisir shows maids making beds, a royal couple at table, and servants attending their masters and mistresses. In one scene the princess is at her dressing table, in another the duke is being shaved by the court barber. On a less exalted plane, there are market scenes, a card game, a musical gathering, an apothecary's shop, a formal garden, shoppers, shopkeepers, a puppet show, clowns, and a fair with booths – a perfect three-dimensional representation of life of that time in a north German court.

The Duchess Dorothea showed Mon Plaisir during her lifetime for the benefit of an orphanage. Happily it has survived and can now be seen (though not without some difficulty) in the Arnstadt Castle Museum, East Germany.

Quite different in style from Mon Plaisir is the elegant wooden Gontard town house in the Stadtische Historische Museum, Frankfurt. This house is hard to place because of its mixed background – it is Dutch in origin with German influences. It came from Holland to Frankfurt in 1748 and was passed down through several generations who all added to it, so it is a mixture of styles and dates. It has six rooms on two floors. The central hall has a balustraded staircase rising to the top-floor hall and on the left of the hall downstairs is a storeroom crammed with dried provisions, pickles, bottles, and smoked meats. On the right, a family sits at a meal in a Victorian-looking dining room. A crowded kitchen, a top hall containing a press, and a bedroom with a large stove occupy the top floor.

DUTCH DOLLS' HOUSES

In Holland, the tradition of fine cabinet baby houses, few of them making any attempt to look like real houses, continued. Sara Ploos Van Amstel (neé Sara Rothé) was responsible for one famous baby house, now in the beautiful Gemeente Museum at The Hague.

Sara's husband was a wealthy merchant, so she could well afford to indulge her passion for baby houses. She acquired three old doll cabinets at auction in 1743 and took rooms from these (notably the lying-in room and kitchen) and put them into this one cabinet. It is very large, 6 ft (1.8 m) high, 2 ft 7 in (0.79 m) deep and 2 ft 7 in (0.79 m) wide, with a three-drawer base.

The cabinet is furnished on three levels. The rooms are all in boxes which have had borders or frames added to give them some sort of unity. Some of the boxes belonged to the artist David Van Der Plaats, and it was he who painted the murals on the music-room walls, some of the elaborately patterned canvas carpets and ceilings, and probably the landscape with cows in the curio room on the top level.

To quote the museum's excellent guide book: "Mrs Van Amstel renewed a great part of the furnishings of the music room. She ordered 'a plain table in the new fashion, having a drawer, fl. 23, six English chairs upholstered in red velvet, this together being thirteen guilders and five stivers; two ivory small round tables painted to resemble wood'."

Sara also had the porcelain room on the second level altered. It contains opaque glass painted to look like the Chinese blue-and-white porcelain which was so popular in homes of the period. Here are Chinese shapes made in China for the European market, with an occasional typically Chinese shape given a Dutch handle or spout. In

A detail of the music room (LEFT) in the Van Amstel cabinet – a games table on which are a chess board, packs of cards, and dice. The kitchen (BELOW) is occupied by three very well-dressed wax-doll servants – the housekeeper, a maid, and the cook (or, perhaps, another maid).

the middle of the porcelain room is a typical 18th-century collector's tortoiseshell cabinet, its drawers containing shells set in wax.

There are two more curio cabinets in the art and curio room on the top level, one holding shells and rolls of paper, the other medals, and again it is interesting to encounter full-sized, similar cabinets as you walk round the museum.

The garden room is less spectacular than that of the Utrecht house. It has perspective views showing a typical garden in which severe lines and clipped hedges complement the architecture of the period. For the making of the marble floor and coloured pedestal, Sara paid fl. 24. On the pedestal stands a "statue of lead made by Mr Sluys and gilded by Mr Buttener".

The kitchen is a mixture made up from items previously bought, with things added by Sara. It has a very pretty set of blue Delft plates in a large rack and a full complement of household utensils – egg rack, footwarmers, pestle and mortar, knife sharpener, and large pewter plates in the cupboard at the back of the room.

Perhaps even more elaborate is the dolls' house known as the

In the garden room of the Van Amstel cabinet (RIGHT) *a wax doll sits with her attentive dog in front of a mural depicting a typical formal garden vista of the period.*

OPPOSITE: *details of two rooms from the German town-in-miniature, Mon Plaisir (see pages 43–4). In a bedroom* (TOP) *a mother is being presented with her baby and in the apothecary's shop* (BOTTOM) *a clearly hungover customer is waiting to be served.*

The twelve exquisitely furnished and equipped rooms of the Blaaw house.

Blaaw house, in the Frans Hals museum, Haarlem, which also once belonged to Sara Ploos Van Amstel. The exterior of the house with its many-paned windows marks a big step from cabinet to representation of real house. Over the front door are the intertwined initials JPVASR (Jacob Ploos Van Amstel Sara Rothé). The house itself contains twelve rooms (if you count the halls) on four floors and is filled with exquisitely made silver by foremost silversmiths, basketware, miniature paintings by leading painters, tables, chairs, glassware, pottery, and a full set of wax figures.

At the bottom of the house is the working kitchen with cupboards, a meat "hastener" before the fire, china colanders, and a silver meat chopper. A particularly realistic-looking cat adds a homely touch in the absence of a cook.

The centre room is a storeroom and on the right is the dining room with a "convenience" in the cupboard at the back (a novel place for it), a cupboard full of ivory and blue-and-white china, a table set with silver on an immaculate white cloth, and a side table with silver serving spoons and silver bowls. Painted chinoiserie scenes decorate the walls.

On the next level is the spectacular silver room, sparkling with the silver for which the Dutch were renowned – trays, coffee pots, porringers, and candlesticks – all displayed in a recess at the rear of the room. The floors here were painted by Buttener and the ceilings by Jacob de Wit. There are portraits of English royalty in the shape of William and Mary, Queen Anne, and George I. A central hall is dominated by a large lantern underneath which stands a very small maidservant. On the right is the study of Dr Ludeman, astrologer and physician, containing a wealth of interesting things, such as a tray containing two silver insects pulling a tiny silver coach, a chest (with a complicated locking mechanism in the lid) full of money bags, a box of medicine bottles, an ivory hourglass, scales, a curious crystal skull topped by a silver crown (a *memento mori*), and Dr Ludeman himself, wearing a cap and silk gown over his outdoor clothes. Paintings by Buttener depict scenes from the doctor's life. In one of them the doctor seems to be visiting a patient stricken with gout.

A music room containing a piano and more silver objects, another hall, and the inevitable lying-in room with mother, a midwife with her knitting, and two babies almost invisible under their coverlets, occupy the third level. On top are laundry rooms and what must be a man's bedroom, judging from the guns on the gun rack, the ivory arrows, and the map cabinet containing large flat folders tied with ribbon.

Another 18th-century house in the Rijksmuseum has an opening front with many windows and steps up to a well-proportioned door. The façade is kept closed in the museum, but the house is well lit from the inside, enabling visitors to peep into the simply furnished rooms and see the pretty staircase running up the centre of the house, the storerooms, the low-ceilinged kitchen, the reception rooms with their plaster decorations, painted walls, and fine mantelpieces, the nursery with its

OVERLEAF
A corner of the lying-in room of the sumptuous Van Amstel house (LEFT). *The elegantly dressed mother sits beside the baby, which is almost invisible in its cradle. The more coarsely featured midwife sits in the background with her knitting. In the music room of the house* (RIGHT) *a gentleman sits beside a painted clavier with what seems to be a decanter in a silver wine cooler at his feet. The realistic looking carpet is painted on the wooden floor.*

high chair, the bedroom, and the laundry, all of which lack the detail of the other two houses in the museum.

A less ambitious but very charming little 18th-century Dutch cabinet house can be seen at the Simon van Gijn museum in Dordrecht. It has only five rooms in three separate cases, one on top of the other, and it measures about 5 ft 7 in (1.7 m) high plus its 2 ft 4 in (0.7 m) stand. The bedroom is on the top floor, a large drawing room takes up the whole of the middle floor, and a kitchen and storeroom are on the bottom level. Alterations were made to the house in the 19th century and it is possible that the bright-eyed Queen Anne style dolls, about 8 in (20 cm) high, have had their heads repainted. The kitchen is typically Dutch, with its frilled mantelshelf and pewter plates, ivory sweeping brush, coffee mill, and pump in the corner. (Wealthy households usually had two pumps, one for spring water and one for rainwater.) Housekeeper and cook take their ease at the back of the room, footwarmers at the ready. In the storeroom is a brass "doofpot", into which coals were put at night as a fire precaution. (A doofpot, and indeed most of the items in the baby-house kitchen, can be seen full-sized in the full-size kitchen at the Simon van Gijn museum.)

The kitchen of the 18th-century cabinet house in the Simon van Gijn museum, occupied by a Queen Anne-style doll sitting at the fireside – a housekeeper in a print dress.

There is an 18th-century Dutch dolls' house in the Strong Museum in New York. The Art Museum at Denver, Colorado, has an 18th-century Dutch baroque house in a glass-fronted cabinet (page 54). This has a roof garden and three rooms (kitchen, sitting room, and bedroom) with period dolls. It was acquired complete in 1921 by Dr Rosenburg, who added only a few pieces to it.

ENGLISH DOLLS' HOUSES

Meanwhile in England there was a great and growing interest in baby houses. Even royalty dabbled in the new craze – Frederick, Prince of Wales, son of George II, was said to have taken up dolls' houses as a hobby after visiting the Duchess Dorothea's Mon Plaisir. It seems a pity that nothing remains to be seen of this early royal interest, when many of the later royals left their mark on the world of dolls' houses.

Baby houses in England were sometimes based on real houses, with opening fronts and staircases, but even if they were not, they certainly looked like houses, not cabinets. Some baby houses were actually played with by children, for they were not teaching aids like the German ones, nor were they display cabinets like those in Holland.

The small drawing room or boudoir on the top floor of the Simon van Gijn house is decorated with prints (which are probably later than 18th century) and furnished with a glass-fronted cabinet, two chairs, a table, and a stool. A footwarmer, a kettle, and a candlestick have been left on the carpet.

*The sitting room and kitchen of a rare
Dutch cabinet house at Denver, Colorado
(see page 53). The sitting-room chandelier
resembles the one in the drawing room
shown opposite.*

In a corner of the drawing room of the Simon van Gijn museum house, elegantly dressed dolls are seated at a small table – the man with a silver tobacco jar at his elbow. The walnut long-case clock behind them is embellished with ormolu decoration.

Vivien Greene, in *English Dolls' Houses of the Eighteenth and Nineteenth Centuries*, says: "The best guide in dating a baby house is the thickness of the walls and the look of solidity.... Look for evidence of painstaking carpentry: carefully made roof-ridges, for instance, and separately carved tiles. Hand-made iron handles at the sides can confirm tentative dating...."

The less important ones were small, unpainted wooden structures with plenty of architectural detail, such as the travelling house from Vivien Greene's own collection at the Rotunda, Oxford, which dates from the early 18th century. Made in mahogany with mother-of-pearl inlay, it is only 17 in (43 cm) high and would have travelled comfortably in a coach.

Another early mahogany house (1730–40) from the collection is interesting in that it shows the transition from cabinet house to dolls' house – the stand is still important but the house is clearly meant to resemble a real house and has good architectural detail. There are no chimneys and the staircase is in one piece and designed to lift out, making it a useful place in which to hide jewellery while travelling.

There were even smaller houses, as we can see from the paintings of George Moreland, who died in 1804. His picture *Domestic Happiness* shows a child with a tiny dolls' house shaped like a dog kennel with windows and door, hardly big enough to hold one room, and his *The Young Nurse and Quiet Child* shows a small girl rocking her doll in a cradle, with a similar small house in the foreground.

The more important dolls' houses were bigger and heavier altogether. Designed by architects, their exteriors were carved to resemble brickwork and they had a great deal of detail in the shape of fine staircases, columns, architraves, rusticated masonry, glazing bars, and so on. Rooms were low, unlike those of Victorian houses. Inside were ornate mantelpieces, steel or brass grates, brass fenders, and carved niches for ornaments. This was the age of painters Devis, Gainsborough, and Reynolds, when wealthy gentlemen went on the Grand Tour of Europe and came back to beautify their country seats. The English baby houses reflect their owners' cultured tastes, which were translated into wood by cabinet makers, by estate carpenters, and by craftsmen.

Nostell Priory baby house is a perfect example of this grand style. The house was commissioned in about 1735 by Sir Rowland Winn and designed by his architect, James Paine, who based it on the real Nostell Priory in West Yorkshire, though it is not an exact copy. The unpainted exterior of the house, which opens and closes by sliding its two halves together, is a lovely piece of craftsmanship. The pedimented windows and doors all have working locks and handles. This attention to detail is repeated inside the house. The rooms contain meticulously carved panelling and mouldings; each fender is separately designed and even the firedogs differ from room to room. The perfect period furniture is said to have been made by Thomas Chippendale, who had as a young man lived not far away, at Otley. There are nine rooms in this huge house, which measures 6 ft 10½ in (2.1 m) × 6 ft 3½ in (2 m) × 2 ft 6¾ in (0.8 m). The rooms vary in size, those at the top of the house being slightly smaller in height than the rest, and all the rooms vary in width. The house is populated by a family and servants (cook, nursemaid, and footmen) and, as was the custom at that time, the family dolls were made of wax, the servant dolls of wood. The rooms were decorated by Lady Winn and her sister, who obviously took a great interest in the dolls' house – it seems probable that this house was an amusement for adults rather than children, who in any case could not have reached the top rooms. Floors throughout are of polished wood, though there are a few rugs, as was the fashion in real houses of the period.

An early-18th-century travelling house from Vivien Greene's collection at the Rotunda, Oxford.

The rooms on the top floor are all panelled and decorated in pale blue with floral and white hangings for one bedroom and plain yellow for the other. The third room on this floor is a dressing room, furnished with a fine chest of drawers, a handsome firescreen, several chairs, and a large landscape painting. A wax doll occupies this room, so she must be one of the family, though she is not as grandly dressed as the other family dolls.

The middle floor contains a splendid drawing room decorated with découpage scenes on a yellow background. Lady Winn and her sister probably cut out paper prints from books that were especially published about this time for the craft of japanning, which was very popular with ladies of leisure. A yellow tone usually results from the several coats of varnish that are applied to the cut-out paper designs. The table is set for tea and there is a Chinese lacquered cabinet against one wall. Some of the gilt decoration is also made of paper.

The centre room, another bedroom, almost overwhelmed by its red velvet bed hangings and panels, has a walnut bureau, a long-case clock, a white quilted-silk bed cover, a white fireplace, and two paintings. Next to the bedroom is a small parlour with brightly coloured Chinese wallpaper patterned with birds and blossom. On the ground floor is the panelled dining room, with a liveried servant standing by the door, and a panelled entrance hall furnished with carved chairs, a table, two more paintings, and a very nice floor of dark and light wood. Finally, there is the kitchen, which is rather small for a house of this size, with arched ovens at the back and a cradle-like grate made of horizontal iron bars fixed to four legs. This is high and broad across the front, for ease of roasting. The width of such a fireplace could be adjusted by moving the sides or cheeks, winding them in and out by a rack and pinion mechanism. There are rows of shining plates and more dishes are on the dresser and in a plate-drying rack. The chef is wearing a pink-and-white hat decorated with a pom-pom. Lurking in the corner is a strange animal, which may be about to be attacked by the chef. An ivory mouse is hiding under the table.

The Nostell Priory baby house is a masterpiece, but even more elegant is the Uppark baby house. If an author is allowed to have a favourite dolls' house, then this is mine. The house was brought to its new home, Uppark in the south of England, by Sarah Lethieullier when she went there as the bride of Sir Matthew Fetherstonhaugh in 1747, although it was probably made earlier. The house, standing 4 ft 9 in (0.8 m) on a 2 ft 4 in (0.7 m) pediment, has been left untouched and is a time-capsule of life in a great country house 250 years ago. Its interior is a perfect example of Queen Anne style; its exterior is ornamented with classical figures and Corinthian and Ionic columns.

The three rooms on each of three floors all open individually from the front, and there are delicate architectural details such as brass door locks and knobs, panelled walls, and marble fireplaces with brass firegrates. Beds are rare French-style "angel" beds (so-called because

In the Nostell Priory baby house the third room on the middle floor is a parlour (OPPOSITE). *It contains a fine bureau-bookcase, its desk open to reveal a complex of pigeonholes. The chairs are in Chippendale style.*

they are not supported by four posts and seem to "fly" from the ceilings). Mirrors are plain and unadorned and the furnishings simple and graceful, giving support to the view that they probably date a little earlier than the actual baby house.

The dolls'-house inhabitants conform to the early 18th-century convention – servants have wooden heads, while the gentry upstairs are made of wax and dressed in elegant clothes. Each lady wears the correct cap and gown and even has on the right number of petticoats. The dining room is laid for a meal, with silver table settings under a silver chandelier. There is an arched niche painted blue and gold and containing ornaments at the back of the room.

Oak was used for all the ground-floor furniture, walnut for the first floor, and ivory for the top floor. To the left of the dining room, the family is sitting in the well-appointed parlour taking tea. The gentleman of the house wears fashionable clothes and a powdered wig and carries a sword at his side, for it was still the custom for men to carry them at this time.

The third room on the centre floor is the lying-in room; it contains two ladies, one in bed and one sitting in the foreground, and two babies in a cradle. It was once thought that this scene represented a mother

The Nostell Priory house with its front opened to disclose the arrangement of rooms.

with twins and their nurse, but as upper-class 18th-century ladies did not breast-feed their babies, the figures could represent a new mother and her wet nurse, with the nurse's child and the new arrival sharing the same cradle. At the side of the room is a dressing or toilet table, so called because it was covered with a "toile" or cover to protect the top. From this the word "toilette" evolved to describe a table at which a lady would sit to do her face and from this comes our modern world "toilet".

The paintings throughout the house are perfect replicas of those found in full-sized great houses – landscapes in the Italian manner, pictures of other big country houses, cattle and sporting scenes, all painted on wood. Some of them may have been painted by Lady Sarah herself, for she was an accomplished artist; others may have been by George Romney, who also painted Nelson's Emma Hamilton. They say that Emma once lived at Uppark and that as a girl of 15 she caught the eye of Harry Fetherstonhaugh, son of Sarah, and entertained him and his friends by dancing on the table there. It is touching to think that Emma, little more than a child, might have taken a few minutes from her duties to play with the dolls' house at the great country house in which she was living.

Another two mid-18th century baby houses in London museums

The drawing room of the Nostell Priory house, with its fine fireplace. No two fireplaces in the house are alike.

In the dining room (LEFT) of the Uppark house liveried servants wait to serve the family, and the table – walnut, like the rest of the furniture – is laid with fine glass and silver. In the kitchen (ABOVE) the cook, surrounded by huge pewter plates and heavy copper pans, is hard at work preparing the meal.

OPPOSITE: *the splendid classical front of the Uppark baby house (see pages 58–61).*

follow the English tradition in that although they are on stands they resemble real houses and are not just boxes for costly miniatures.

The Tate baby house (named after its donor, Mrs Walter Tate), dated 1760, is at the Bethnal Green Museum of Childhood. This handsome construction on its own stand, smaller than Uppark or Nostell, is memorable for its architecturally accurate exterior, with a double staircase to the pedimented front door and good windows and balustrading. It was based on a Dorset house of the period. Modernization was carried out in the following century and sash windows replace the original ones. (Large windows became popular in the early 19th century when plate glass was introduced.) The furniture also was updated in 1830, though the house does contain some 18th-century pieces and the interior panelling and the fireplaces are original. The four rooms visible are the bedroom, dining room, and two reception rooms, and there is also a kitchen in the basement.

The architectural detail of the exterior of the Blackett house, which

The arrangement of rooms in the Uppark house. The centre rooms are shallower than those at the sides, to accommodate the staircase at the back of the house. There are three bedrooms on the top floor, a reception room, a dining room, and another bedroom on the middle floor, and a kitchen, hall, and housekeeper's room on the bottom floor. Each room opens independently from the front.

can be seen at the Museum of London, is almost as fine as that of the Tate baby house. It, too, has balustrading and a double staircase to the front door, though it is not as spectacular as that of the Tate. The lower part of the house forms the stand and the front door surround is rusticated, that is, blocks or courses of stone are emphasized by deeply recessed joints. The detail inside does not match up to the exterior. There are only four rooms – a kitchen, a dining room, a parlour, and a bedroom – and again, some items have been added at a later date, although there are some original pieces and the house has the added attraction of retaining its original wax dolls.

The hand-painted wallpaper is pretty, blue with large flowers in the parlour and bedroom and bearing hand-painted classical scenes in panels in the dining room. There are many good pieces of furniture. The parlour has an interesting screen decorated with scenes from Aesop's fables. There is a good supply of pots and pans in the kitchen, where there is a spit-rack and a mechanical jack for roasting meat. The

The Tate baby house, its front door grandly approached by swirling flights of steps.

ABOVE: *the parlour of the Blackett baby house, with its pretty, hand-painted blue floral wallpaper.*

OPPOSITE: *the King's Lynn dolls' house, with its six rooms restored and furnished with pieces in a style appropriate to its period.*

kitchen is presided over by a wax-doll cook, which is unusual for this period. The bedroom has a four-poster bed with tassels at the corners, upon which rests a cushion romantically embroidered with hearts and the words "Unis à Jamais". The lady of the house is placed by the wash bowl and at her feet is a Victorian-looking water can. On a chest of drawers with big brass handles is another bowl and a jug and in the background is a dressing table covered with a "toile", and a mirror.

Unfortunately not all 18th-century English baby houses have survived with their furniture intact. The recently discovered King's Lynn baby house (*c.*1740) had only its original panelling, doors, and fireplaces when it was rescued from obscurity. The house, which measures about 5 ft (1.5 m) in height on its rusticated stand and which bears some resemblance to the Blackett house, has an interesting history. It is a replica in miniature of 27 King Street, King's Lynn, Norfolk, once the home of a Dutch merchant named Flierden and his wife. The baby house was built for their only child, Ann. Mr Flierden, who imported wine and other merchandise and owned a small quay on the river at the bottom of the garden, set up a counting house at 27 King Street. Ann, who died in childbirth at the age of 23, married into

another banking family. Today, the house is the home of the King's Lynn Social History Museum, where one of the exhibits is Ann Flierden's spinet, a modern miniature replica of which is in the music room of the baby house. In the 1920s, a local dignitary gave the baby house to a Torquay children's home run by the Children's Society. Before that it had been kept somewhere in Bath, but it is not known how it got from King's Lynn to Bath. In 1984, the Children's Society initiated the restoration of the house. The work was carried out by Vivien Greene and a group of craftswomen, who furnished the two bedrooms, dining room, music room, kitchen, and counting house with modern furniture in a style that was both suitable to the period and in accord with the Flierdens' Quaker beliefs.

Early though it is, the 18th-century baby house at Strangers' Hall, Norwich, is far removed from the concept of the cabinet house on its own stand. It is a dolls' house to be played with, smaller, more like a house, less grandly architectural than some of the others described and sturdily built to withstand the destructiveness of children.

The original house of which the King's Lynn dolls' house is a model – 27 King Street, now the home of the King's Lynn Social History Museum.

The solid wooden house with carrying handles is painted to look like brickwork, with stone quoins (emphasized stones) at the edges. Most of the sash windows have their original glazing bars. Much of the furniture in the three rooms (bedroom, parlour, and kitchen) is Victorian. The kitchen (page 71) is the most interesting room. If the date of the house is, as seems likely, 1720, then the range must be later, for it has spaces on either side occupied by boiler and oven – a style that only occurs after 1780. The racks holding the horizontal spits over the fireplace are probably original; they would have been pointless used with this range, which has half its cooking power taken up by boiler and oven. The clockwork spit-turning mechanism, similar to those in the Blackett, Uppark, and Nostell Priory baby houses, would also have served little purpose with this type of grate.

An interesting piece of equipment is the "hastener" which was placed before the fire with a bottle jack suspended from the bar at the top, the cylinder of the jack remaining above the hastener, the wheel inside revolving with the meat hanging from it on hooks. Cooking progress was monitored through a door at the back and there would have been a dish or a tray underneath the meat to catch the dripping, an essential ingredient for many English dishes. A different type of hastener can be seen in the Nuremberg house at the Bethnal Green Museum of Childhood.

There are many more English baby houses of the 18th century in existence – the Yarburgh baby house at the Castle Museum, York, for one. This was made in about 1751 for the Heslington children and is a sturdy model made for playing with. It consists of nine rooms, each opening independently, on three floors, the size of the rooms decreasing towards the attics. The eldest of the Heslington girls married the famous architect Sir John Vanbrugh in 1719. He was working at nearby Castle Howard from 1701 to 1726 and there is speculation whether he designed this baby house for his future wife's family, but in view of the basic nature of the Yarburgh house and remembering the gracious lines of Castle Howard, it does seem improbable. The inside of the house is as workmanlike as the outside, the doors are fixed closed and unadorned and much of the furniture is of later date, but the fireplaces are original and they have their steel or brass firebaskets. The kitchen has an arched fireplace with a large grate and no side ovens, spit racks, and a clockwork spit-turning mechanism, like that of Nostell Priory.

Cane End house in Vivien Greene's collection at the Rotunda, Oxford, is dated 1756. The house belonged to the Vanderstegen family and is a replica of their real house, Cane End, Reading. The Master himself copied in miniature the Chinese Chippendale he had made for the real house. The brass open-drop door handles have survived as have the dresser and spit rack. Suitable furniture has since gradually been added. Vivien Greene also has a wooden 1720–30 baby house and another, Portobello Road (1700–10), in which there is a chest containing scraps of gowns worn by Queen Charlotte and Queen Victoria.

The elegant, formal lines of the baby house at Strangers' Hall, Norwich.

OPPOSITE: *the simply furnished counting house of the King's Lynn dolls' house.*

TOP LEFT: *the most interesting room of the Strangers' Hall house is the kitchen, with its spit-turning mechanisms, spit racks, and hastener. The firegrate is a later addition.*

*When Vivien Greene bought Cane End house (*LEFT*), she found the beautifully patterned old wood-block printed wallpaper intact beneath more modern paper. The lovely winding staircase linking all three floors was also intact.*

71

OTHER EUROPEAN DOLLS' HOUSES

Returning to the mainland of Europe, France can be mentioned only in passing, since it has little to offer here. Marie Antoinette is supposed to have owned a dolls' house and it would be delightful were there any trace of this. An early dolls' house consisting of only two rooms and dated 1791 is described by Leo Clarétie in one of his books on toys and dolls.

Scandinavian countries can boast one or two 18th-century baby houses. The Dansk Folkemuseum, Copenhagen, has a plain wooden two-storey house with a mansard roof from Hagen, Westphalia. It is handsomely proportioned and opens in one piece to reveal two rooms, both of which are sparsely furnished. The top room contains a four-poster bed and four little carved chairs; the bottom has a large cupboard, shelves with some china, four chairs, and a table.

The Nordiska Museet Stockholm, Sweden, has about thirty dolls' houses in its collection, the oldest of which is the late 17th-century one described in the previous chapter. Their cabinet house, dated 1750, is not a dolls' house at all but a glass-fronted cabinet. It is furnished on four levels, one of which is divided into three rooms. On the bottom

This unusual house, dated about 1790, in the collection of Mrs Maas, was perhaps intended to represent an inn – the George III. It has been restored as a house of four rooms.

The mansard-roofed house from Hagen opens to display only three rooms – a living/dining room, a bedroom, and an attic room for a servant.

Two rooms from the cabinet shown opposite – the elegant ballroom (BELOW) and a small ante-room with a large tiled stove and family portraits on the walls.

level is a kitchen containing a pewter dinner service and a very small cook. On the next level is a bedroom and a boudoir in which sits a regal-looking lady winding wool on a machine. The room next to this appears to be a sort of anteroom, with a large tiled stove in one corner and imposing portraits on the walls. Above this is a ballroom, with a chequerboard floor and a rural scene painted on the walls. Elegant little chairs are ranged along a wall under a row of mirrored candle sconces. The top floor holds a standing mirror, chairs, and a good chest of drawers. There are portraits on the walls, some of them real miniatures.

The Vestlandkse Kunstindustrimuseum, Bergen, Norway, also possesses a charming 18th-century cabinet house, containing chairs and ottomans upholstered in Florentine stitch. It is unusually arranged, with a bedroom and kitchen on the ground floor and on the next floor two reception rooms, one of which has a sophisticated mural on the wall. The kitchen has a rack of pewter plates, a curious wheel-shaped object (which may be a grill) on the wall, and a notched rack which is probably part of a spit, though the oven is so low that you wonder how it worked.

A glass-fronted cabinet (BELOW LEFT), *dated 1750, in Stockholm. The ballroom takes up the whole of the third level ; the ante-room is to the right of the bedroom on the level below. The big kitchen occupies the entire bottom level and has room to display many dishes and plates. In one corner* (BELOW) *there is a dresser and some well-made blue-and-white china.*

The 18th-century cabinet house at Bergen, crammed with furniture, fittings, utensils, and oddments.

The bedroom has a draped bed and there are two hanging fabric items on the wall, one of which may be a sort of hanging cupboard. The sitting-room tables are set with tea things, which are interesting because they resemble the alabaster table and tea things in the Uppark baby house of the same date.

AN AMERICAN DOLLS' HOUSE

The earliest extant dolls' house in the United States is the Van Cortlandt house, which can be seen today in the museum of that name in New York.

Made for a member of the Homans family in 1744, at a time of emerging national identity in the years before the War of Independence, it too has its own separate identity – it has a charmingly unadorned, homely appearance which owes nothing to German, Dutch, or English houses of the same period.

The house is arranged on two floors of two rooms each, the rooms at the top being divided by wooden railings which admit light to the room at the back. Windows are painted on the exterior of the house, which sits on top of a drawer holding toys and spare furniture. All that remains of the original furnishings are the fireplaces and shelves.

MINIATURES

In England, shops supplying furniture for baby houses existed by the mid-18th century and quite a lot of furniture was already being imported from Holland and Germany. Before that there had been workshops where the functions of manufacturer, wholesaler, and retailer were combined and the nature of the goods supplied was often determined by the raw materials in stock, so that a cabinet maker might turn his hand to making little pieces of dolls'-house furniture out of the scraps left over from larger, commissioned pieces. Furniture could also be commissioned from local craftsmen, for a price, and some could be home-made, so it was not too difficult to furnish a baby house.

English baby houses are not as lavishly provided with precious objects as are the Dutch houses, but there is plenty of brass and pewter kitchenware and some silver, as well as glassware and china dishes and tea sets. The alabaster tea service in the housekeeper's room at Uppark is pleasing and the drawing room in the Nostell Priory house has a pretty silver tea service, though it is for its furniture that the house is chiefly distinguished. There is a fine walnut desk in the small parlour, with pigeon holes for letters and detailed handles and keyholes.

Dolls'-house furniture can be dated approximately from when a fashion or style or invention was introduced. Washstands came into being in about 1740, followed closely by shaving mirrors on stands. Embroidered pole screens were fashionable from about 1750; tea services were imported from the East by about 1720, the first to be used

Two Tunbridge-ware pin tables (BELOW) that have found a new use as dolls'-house furniture. The table on the left is by Thomas Barton, best known of all Tunbridge-ware manufacturers, who was in business from 1863 until his death, aged 83, in 1902. The two lignum-vitae castors (ABOVE) were, however, made as miniatures – intended only for dolls'-house tables.

having no handles and being decorated with oriental designs. Stair carpets were unusual until about the mid 19th century.

The wood lignum vitae was much used, often together with ivory, in English 18th-century baby houses, for castors, cruets, knife holders, and bottle coolers. Another distinctive type of English wooden furniture was made in the Tunbridge Wells area from the 17th to the 19th century. Known as Tunbridge ware, it is made from thin sheets of patterned veneer sliced from blocks, built up from thin strips of wood in a variety of colours.

Nuremberg had been the centre of the German toy industry since the 16th century. This came about because the town was a convenient market and distribution point for toymakers in various parts of Germany and because it had a strong tradition of arts and crafts. In the 17th century Nuremberg's speciality was dolls' houses and in the 18th and 19th centuries, kitchens.

The curio room of the Van Amstel house contains two craftsman-made cabinets (BELOW), one holding medals, the other a collection of shells. There are similar cabinets in the Blaauw house. The corner of the Van Amstel porcelain room (OPPOSITE) is lushly mirrored and luxuriously carpeted.

Dutch silversmiths were renowned for their skills at this time. Craftsmen like Van Geffen worked on some of the silver for Sara Ploos Van Amstel's house at Haarlem, a dolls' house which has a special room devoted to silver. Coffee pots, trays, candlesticks, and vessels are all displayed in a recess at the back of the silver room.

The silver in this house is very fine indeed, much of it dating from the previous century, as the rooms had come to Sara second-hand. The lying-in room contains a 17th-century toilet set from the older rooms, including the rather stubby, unmistakably 17th-century, silver candlestick. The dressing-table silver can be compared with the silver gilt toilet set, also in the Gemeente Museum, which was made in The Hague in 1653–8. The housekeeper in the nursery on the top level wears a silver chatelaine holding a knife and fork, needlecase, and silver scissors. In the music room are silver sconces, candlesticks, a waste-paper basket, and fire-irons, a cabinet filled with silver, and another little silver cupboard containing silver toys, which was once in the nursery.

The silver sconces in the music room of the house at The Hague are also of superior quality. Because Dutch silversmiths had such a reputation, their silver was exported to England along with other miniatures, so it is often to be found in the grand English baby houses. After about 1750 such silver was mainly Dutch. Whereas the Dutch made a great variety of things in silver, English silver toys were usually utensils. David Clayton, a well-known English silversmith, made silver toys, but in a larger scale than those made for dolls' houses.

Glass is another feature of the Dutch cabinet houses. The porcelain room of the Amstel house in The Hague contains blue-and-white glass painted to give the impression of porcelain. The music room of the same house contains drinking glasses and a green glass flask with a gold stopper. The Sara Ploos Van Amstel house contains trays bearing all kinds of glassware – rummers, goblets, and beer glasses.

The Dutch dolls' houses also have furniture as fine as any found in English baby houses of the period, as can be seen from the cabinets in the curio room of The Hague house – though as we have seen, some of this furniture was made in England.

Miniatures from the kitchen of the Blaaw house – the kitchen cat (BELOW), a doofpot (BOTTOM LEFT), and (BOTTOM RIGHT) a group of useful items – a portable spit, cooking pots, tongs, a candlestick, and an oil lamp.

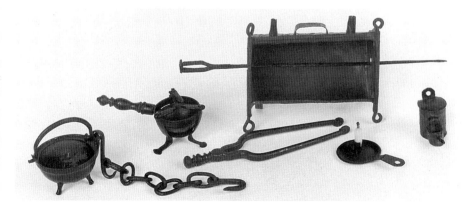

THE 19TH CENTURY

By the early 1800s the fashionable adult craze for baby houses had faded. Dolls' houses started to become strongly made playthings, silverware being replaced by practical wood and pottery, graciously proportioned rooms and staircases giving way to divisions into three or four rooms. Fronts no longer opened on to separate rooms but in one or two sections, windows had single panes, and, since dolls' houses ceased to contain valuables, it was no longer necessary to fit locks.

As Vivien Greene points out in *English Dolls' Houses*, dolls' houses of the 1850s and 1860s were characterized by elaborate and well-made façades, displaying pillars, mouldings, and rustication, but by badly proportioned interiors, scamped detail, and low, unpanelled doors. By the end of the century, walls had become thinner, paper was splitting over the cracks in the cheap wood used to form the walls, there was only the most perfunctory indication of stone or brick, and workmanship was expended on windows of unpleasant proportions. Beautiful stairs were a thing of the past. The kitchen was usually the pleasantest room. Mass-produced Victorian dolls' houses always have rooms too high for their size and late-Victorian mass-manufactured houses are the worst in this respect. Smaller dolls' houses were no longer display pieces; they offered minimal style and decoration and were only realistic enough to satisfy a child's modest requirements. There were exceptions of course, and some hand-made houses had façades and interiors as aesthetically pleasing as those of the previous century.

Furnishings of all kinds could be bought easily and cheaply, thanks mainly to the production of the German factories, which exported throughout the world, and what could not be bought could be home-made, for what dolls'-house owner has ever been able to resist making things for her house?

It is not surprising that dolls' houses changed in the 19th century, for the whole world was changing dramatically and dolls' houses are to some extent a barometer of life in the real world. The Industrial Revolution had led to enormous changes – the steam engine had transformed industry and transport, canals and railways came into being, cities grew. With them grew the manufacturing industries.

Dolls' houses became cheaper to buy, so more homes possessed one, and so 19th-century dolls' houses are today commoner than earlier ones. Some things, though, did not change. The gap between rich and poor remained. For the whole of the first half of the century children as young as five or six from poor families were put out to work, but for the children of the middle and upper classes it was a secure world of nannies, nurseries, and good food, a comfortably ordered way of life.

EUROPEAN DOLLS' HOUSES

Germany, renowned for its 17th-century dolls'-house masterpieces, did not excel at the art in the 19th, its manufacturers concentrating chiefly on dolls' rooms (particularly kitchens) and furnishings, which they exported in huge quantities and variety. Catalogues published to illustrate their goods give us some idea of this variety.

There are some 19th-century dolls' houses in German museums, particularly at Sonneburg and Kommern and in the Nuremberg toy museum, which has a pretty, commercially made town house of about 1880 of a fairly common type.

This house has a front which opens in two halves, top and bottom, to reveal a hall with a staircase between the kitchen and the ground-floor bedroom. The staircase leads nowhere, as there are only two rooms

The commercially made 1880 town house in the toy museum at Nuremberg. Its front opens in two halves, top and bottom.

on the top floor – a dining room and a sitting room. The kitchen has a small stove at the back and a large dresser stocked with utensils, while the table is set with plates and a coffee pot. The bedroom has two beds and a marble-topped washstand, and the dining room has a large tree in the background, which suggests that it is Christmas. A tea table is drawn up to a sofa with four additional chairs round it. In the sitting room are a glass-fronted cabinet, several upholstered chairs, and a sideboard full of ornaments.

The proliferation of shops and rooms rather than houses may be due to the lowly status of German girls at this time. In Germany, the family was all-important and women were kept at home to go to church, to bear and raise children, and to cook and work in the house. Toy kitchens would have been a training for a girls' future duties; they would have been seen as educational aids, in a continuation of the Nuremberg-house tradition.

The fact that many Germans, like the French, lived in apartments rather than houses also has a bearing on the scarcity of dolls' houses of this period, as there would have been little space for such large items even if a girl had been thought worthy of such a gift.

Some German dolls' houses have found their way into the collections of other countries, particularly of the United States. There

Beneath its more elaborate decoration, this town house in Munich is of the same fairly common type (and of about the same date) as the one opposite.

is, for example, a German town house of 1890 in The Strong Museum, New York.

Another, lighter, style of German commercially made house appeared towards the end of the 19th century and continued up until about World War I. This was the French-looking, mansard-roofed style of house, as seen in the 1880 example on page 83. It seems to have been a universal and long-lived style, for one very similar appeared in the American Schwartz toy-shop catalogue of 1931.

The house opposite is dated about 1900 and has been identified by the owner Mrs Barbara Andrew as being made by Christian Hacker, a Nuremberg toymaker. It bears the trade mark he registered in 1875 – the intertwined initials "CH" with a little crown on top. The house opens in two sections, the roof lifts off for access to attic bedrooms, and the whole thing takes to pieces in four sections. In this version, the centre rooms are without a staircase but in others a staircase runs right up the centre of the house or stops at the first floor. This particular house was purchased empty and has been refurnished by the owner, but the dresser and large fireplace are original and are typical of this type of house. Both are edged with dark blue line – a style already seen in the kitchen of the 1880 Nuremberg house (see page 82), which seems to point to a German rather than French origin for this type of house.

There is in the Munich Stadtmuseum a very unusual dolls' house, called Zintl's house, which is really one huge store. Rooms containing neatly stacked fabrics are guarded by assistants standing behind long counters and the windows in the fronts of the house, which swing open, are filled with linen, rows of little jackets, undergarments, hats, and carpets (see pages 86, 87). This is dated 1875–80.

It was hardly to be expected that 19th-century Holland could turn up another Sara Ploos Van Amstel with her money, energy, and enthusiasm for the miniature, but there is a very fine, probably late-19th-century Dutch dolls' house in the Gemeente Museum in The Hague, a house which is filled with good furniture and objects in silver, ivory, and porcelain, altogether a worthy inheritor of the baby-house tradition (pages 88–9).

There are six rooms in this excellently finished house. On the ground floor left is a typical Dutch kitchen, with a frilled mantelshelf of the old style covering an iron stove. On the left, under the window, cook is busy by the sink and there is a side cupboard crammed with glass jugs, pottery bowls, and an ivory cruet. A small metal bread bin, a wicker carpet beater, and a wicker basket containing dish towels fill the foreground. On the wall is a dazzling array of shining metal cooking utensils. A table is laid for coffee with silver coffee pot, cups, and saucers and three chairs with rush seats are drawn up to the table, in front of which is something that looks like a metal footwarmer. Other details include bellows and two tiny Chianti bottles in baskets.

The hall is spacious, furnished with a Chinese lacquer screen and Chinese figures, a corner cupboard holding pottery and glass, an ivory

OPPOSITE: *the Hacker house with its front half-opened to show the ground-floor rooms – kitchen, hall, and dining room. The kitchen dresser and fireplace are lined in dark blue, a style seen also in the house on page 82.*

chess table, and a carved religious figure. A staircase rises to the first floor. A comfortable chair with a newspaper on it is drawn up to the fireplace and there is a leather-bound book on the low table. A third room on the ground floor is furnished as a study, with velvet curtains drawn against the cold, a silver birdcage suspended from the ceiling, and gleaming silver candlesticks, jugs, ornaments, miniatures, and pictures giving it an air of prosperity.

In the drawing room over the study, the elegant lady of the house is taking tea with a visitor. She sits in an armchair, tea things before her on a silver tray. There are some delightful pieces of silver scattered about, a chest of drawers, ornaments, and old paintings on the walls. The carved staircase in the top hall continues up to the attic, whence a maid is descending carrying a pile of cloths. Part of the hall is curtained off to form a small sitting room. On the left is a bedroom containing a cabinet, a dressing table, etchings, a small bed with lace coverlet, and a marble fireplace. The house presents a graphic picture of life in a prosperous Dutch house of the late 19th or early 20th century.

The Strong Museum, New York, also has an elegant Dutch house

Zintl's house (see page 84) is less a dolls' house than a well-stocked drapery store (RIGHT AND OPPOSITE, LEFT).

which formerly stood in the lobby of the Hotel des Pays Bas in Amsterdam. It is furnished with Hinderloopen dining-room furniture, lace curtains, a silver tea service and candelabra, and delicate Delft china.

From time to time, interesting dolls' houses can be found in auction rooms, such as the 1890 house which appeared at Sotheby's not long ago. It was in the Dutch style, though it is not possible to say definitely that it was made in Holland. It had a gabled roof and a base containing a pull-out drawer, not for toys, but to hold the garden. The door was protected by a galleried porch and was flanked by windows. The house was quite small, 2 ft 6 in (0.7 m) high, and 1 ft 6½ in (0.5 m) wide, and had a side opening to reveal two rooms, each with a fireplace and contemporary wallpaper.

French manufacturers concentrated on dolls' rooms rather than houses because, like the Germans, the French tended to live in apartments and space was restricted. French children were not shut away in nurseries with their nannies, as were English children, and not many *mamans* would have wanted a dolls' house taking up space in their

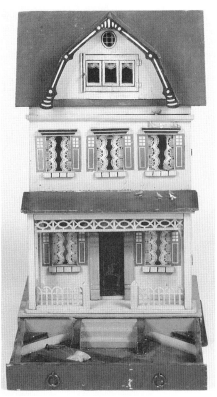

ABOVE: *the Dutch-style painted wooden house, dated 1890, sold by Sotheby's.*

This superbly furnished house in the Gemeente Museum, The Hague, gives a wonderfully detailed picture of life in a well-appointed Dutch house of the period. On the ground floor are a study, hall, and kitchen and on the top floor a drawing room, another hall, and a bedroom.

drawing room. This means that there are not many examples to be seen in the museums, though the Musée des Arts et Traditions Populaires in Paris has a late-19th-century house of the Christian Hacker type and the Musée des Arts Décoratifs in Paris has an attractive and fully furnished 1840 house with double front door, arched windows, and metal grille work. The same museum also has a very unusual Spanish or Portuguese 19th-century dolls' house, which is a display piece rather than a toy and which owes nothing to any tradition of dolls' houses so far encountered. It consists of a two-tiered box with a sort of pagoda on top. The bottom tier holds a dining room containing a well-laid table and bamboo chairs, the wall decorated with a mural of the baptistry, cathedral, and leaning tower of Pisa. A side room is decorated with Gothic arches and could be

The Spanish or Portuguese 19th-century house in the Musée des Arts Décoratifs, Paris.

mistaken for a chapel were it not for a basket chair occupying a lot of space in the middle of the room. Upstairs is a salon decorated with nicely painted murals of country and sea scenes, where a family is seated on French Empire furniture. There is no fireplace, the space where it would be being filled by a mirror and a straight-backed couch with long, round cushions.

Like the Germans, the French exported some dolls' houses, and collectors in England have some across several of the type shown on page 93 which dates from about 1880. This French seaside villa has two rooms and lithographed bricks and wallpaper.

Scandinavian countries produced some delightful dolls' houses in the 19th century, many of which can be seen in their museums. The Nordiska Museet in Stockholm, for example, has a charming 1856 house containing six rooms, all furnished in what can only be described as Swedish Victorian. On the ground floor left is the grandparents' room, where an elderly couple cosily clad in shawls and caps stand among their possessions. Early Victorian prints are on the walls and there is a pretty marble-topped sideboard in the Walterhausen style (for which see page 120). Next to this is the kitchen. Striped Swedish rag rugs cover the floor; the table is laden with food, the side tables with crockery, glass, and silver. Plates are stacked in racks, their pattern obscured by a lace paper trim. In the corner is the cooker surrounded by pots and pans. Brick-patterned papers line the walls. Note how well wrapped-up the cook is, in her thick dress, striped apron, and shawl.

Upstairs in the nursery are three children with their nurse. The

The kitchen in the 1856 Emelie Kihlberg house (see page 92) in the Nordiska Museet, Stockholm.

91

walls here are decorated with framed family photographs, as is the parlour next door, where father (in dressing gown and smoking hat) and mother sit with yet another child. More photographs adorn the walls and there is a statue of an angel in one corner. In the music room above, two young ladies, as warmly clothed as the rest of the family, are talking. It seems odd that there is no sign of heating in the house, apart from the kitchen stove, but it does account for all the warm clothing.

This dolls' house was arranged by Mrs Emelie Kihlberg of Gothenburg for her ten children and three stepchildren in the 1860s. It was kept in the children's room and they were allowed to look at it, hands behind backs, only when mother opened the door!

Copenhagen, so closely associated with the great storyteller Hans Andersen, is appropriately the home of several 19th-century dolls' houses, some of them in Legoland, a place dolls'-house enthusiasts are likely to be visiting to see Titania's Palace (see page 146).

Carlsro (1870–75) has the same arched roof as the Dutch-style house sold by Sotheby's and it has seven rooms, staircase, hall, and toilet. "Grandmother's dolls' house", also at Legoland, dates from about the same period, and the former owner, collector Estrid Faurholt, tells how she was given this, her grandmother's, house. Her mother sent her to the bathroom to fetch a towel, and when she went in, she saw a dolls' house.

> I ran out into the kitchen and shouted that now I knew what I was going to have for Christmas. "No, No," mother said. "That's for little Ellen living upstairs. She must not see it before Christmas. Therefore her parents have hidden it down here."
>
> Oh, how I cried under my blankets every night when no one could see me. Then came Christmas day.
>
> Everyone received Christmas presents except me. As soon as I had told my mother about this injustice, she drew the big portières of our parlour with a strange gleam in her eyes. Here stood the doll's house that had belonged to my grandmother when she was a child. The delightful light-blue kitchen still smelled of fresh paint. The little furniture and dolls were very nicely put in their places. Everything was just so wonderful and delightful.
>
> I honestly believe that the shock of happiness I had has followed me the rest of my life. And that this my first doll's house also has followed me throughout my life together with other houses and dolls which my husband and I have collected on countless travels here in Denmark.

This charming story must strike a chord in the hearts of all of us who love dolls' houses.

While you are in Copenhagen, you could also visit the Dansk Folkemuseum, which has more than twenty dolls' houses. One of them has already been described (page 72); another, named Villa Olga, dated 1884, is a tall, narrow building, over 6 ft (1.8 m) high and 3 ft (0.9 m) wide, with ten windows on the front, two of which are gable windows. It is in the Danish Renaissance style, with the bricks framed in granite blocks that are the hallmark of the style here imitated in wood. Inside there are four floors, the top and bottom floor opening separately, the middle two floors opening together. The bottom floor (the cellar) contains two storerooms, one of them almost filled by a roller press. On the ground floor is a kitchen, on the third a salon, and on the top a bedroom. The maids' rooms would have been in the attics. The chest in the kitchen is a haybox, rarely seen nowadays but much used in Danish kitchens of the past. The house has a flag pole and these are still to be seen on private houses in Denmark where it is the custom to have a flag raised on your birthday.

A small, but quite elaborate, French balconied seaside villa of about 1880.

The cabinet house known as The Three Sisters dates from 1850 and was originally owned by the Danish royal family. Frederick VIII's cipher as crown prince is painted on the top of the house, which was bought at auction by Dorothea Baumann. She restored it with meticulous attention to authenticity of period and presented it to the museum in 1945. Tall Danish porcelain stoves like those seen in the Legoland houses are much in evidence in the drawing room and in the study on the first floor.

The Finnish National Museum, the Museovirasto, Helsinki, has several dolls' houses, the earliest of which, dated 1830, is a mixture of styles and sizes. It consists of three levels in a cabinet and in spite of its name, Ramsay Grano, and a tartan curtain in the kitchen, has no Scottish connections. The kitchen is filled with many objects, some of them more than twice the size of the inhabitants, who are sitting by a wine barrel and a wine flask, clearly in a happy frame of mind. A huge iron and large cooking pots cover the surface of the stove and at the back of the kitchen is a rack of very large plates and two enormous tin trays decorated with Victorian scenes.

The assortment of heavy wooden furniture in the rest of the house indicates that it has been put together haphazardly by several succeeding generations.

Another house in the same museum was made for a merchant's daughter, Aina Friedman, in Raahe in about 1860. Much of its furniture

was produced locally, but on the middle floor you can see a pleasing little Walterhausen writing desk and in the parlour is a well-made corner bookcase. The museum booklet points out that the manufacture of dolls'-house furniture did not begin in this country until the last part of the 19th century so this early Finnish furniture was either home-made or imported, probably from Germany. The house seems very crowded, not only because of the size of the dolls and some of the furniture in relation to the rooms but also because of the overwhelming wallpapers, particularly those on the ground floor.

OPPOSITE: *the tall, narrow Villa Olga* (TOP) *with* (BOTTOM) *its salon filled with heavy stuffed velvet chairs, a cupboard, a whatnot in one corner, and a stove in the other.*

The Hallberg house, dated 1890, in the Museovirasto, Helsinki. It has four rooms – a reception room, a bedroom, a kitchen, and a dining room.

95

There are several 19th-century dolls' houses in the Historische Museum in Basel, Switzerland, the most famous of which is a five-storey house made in 1850 by Basel artist Ludwig Adam Kelterborn for his three daughters. This very detailed house in a cabinet has an attic with a laundry and storage room, six other rooms, and cellars, as well as a large central staircase with doors leading on to balconies.

ENGLISH DOLLS' HOUSES

Nineteenth-century English dolls' houses give a good, if idealized, view of the life of the country's more prosperous citizens at that time. Here are the toy-filled nurseries, the bustling kitchens, the well-laid tables, the over-furnished drawing rooms, and the comfortable bed-rooms known to middle-and upper-class couples, together with their numerous children, relatives, and servants. Dolls' houses were once again fashionable, not only as collectors' showpieces (though there are several of these), but as childrens' toys. Queen Victoria's dolls' house, for example (in the Museum of London), was a very ordinary little flat-fronted affair, two-roomed and furnished with the English and imported German furniture available in the toy shops of the early 19th century. The young Victoria also had a cardboard peepshow in the shape of a little house. It had a brick façade, an ornate front door with an open pediment, and two windows with semi-circular arches on the ground floor and five plain windows on the top. No description is given of the show to be peeped at inside.

Later in the century another royal child had her own dolls' house, which can be seen in the same museum as Queen Victoria's. She was the Princess of Teck, later to become Queen Mary, and her quite ordinary house is still arranged as it was when she was a child. Besides the halls there are six rooms, and they are full of commercially made furniture. As we shall see, Queen Mary never lost her interest in dolls' houses and in later life she was a keen collector of miniatures, dropping in to antique shops whose owners learned to dread a royal visit, for it was only etiquette to offer as a gift any small items which took Her Majesty's eye.

As a report of the same period in the London *Daily Telegraph* (quoted by Flora Gill Jacobs in *A History of Dolls' Houses*) tells us: "Toy warehouses are full of all the miniature goods and chattels which would be required for the most luxurious doll's house of the ordinary type. Admirably pretty upholstery, glass and chinaware and drapery of this sort are made in England and France. The Germans excel in the construction of Lilliputian crockery, kitchen utensils and imitation fruits and viands. A wagon-load of such articles could be obtained from Houndsditch in half an hour, and a doll's house as big as a cabinet piano could be swiftly furnished."

A delightful early English house which bears this out is at Audley End in Essex. It is a roughly constructed toy dated about 1820–40 and it illustrates the transition from the splendid Georgian houses to the mass-produced nursery toys of the late-Victorian period. Pauline Flick,

OPPOSITE: *Aina Friedman's house is given a faintly blowsy look by its out-of-scale furniture and wallpaper with over-sized patterns.*

97

who helped to survey the house and furniture, wrote a scholarly account of it in *The Antique Collector* in 1984:

> The flat front, painted to resemble brick, has three rows of plain windows and a central frame for a now-vanished door, with a hipped "Tile" roof and two chimneys. Nowadays this façade is seldom seen, for the house opens at the rear and so has to be placed back to front against a wall if the rooms are to be accessible.
>
> There is no staircase, though all the rooms have good doors and well-moulded skirting boards and chair rails. What gives this house its special quality however, is not its architecture but the brilliance of its Regency decoration. The papers on the walls – blue, pea green, rose pink, sharp yellow – were probably intended for lining trunks and boxes, but their tiny motifs made them entirely suitable for doll's houses; as an extra embellishment several of the rooms here are trimmed with borders of embossed gold paper at cornice and dado level. All this glitter and colour was perfectly in tune with the prevailing fashion for spectacular furnishings in the real world. Lord Brougham, for example, chose papers of "bright crimson" and "sky blue enlivened by a trellis work pattern of silver" for his bed and dressing room, while Napoleon, some believe, died from arsenical poisons emanating from the bright green wallpaper of his lonely St Helena bedchamber.
>
> As in most doll houses, the furniture at Audley End is a mixture of commercially-produced and home-made pieces. The fine gilt overmantels in the main reception rooms were certainly made by professional craftsmen, as were the full length pier glasses set between the windows. Six rooms have fireplaces with elegant brass grates, one being modelled on the "Bath" pattern so often found in real bedrooms of the early 19th century.
>
> Few doll's houses in England can equal Audley End's display of a very desirable type of pressed tin furniture with a characteristic ginger coloured finish usually described – thanks to Mrs Graham Greene, the first writer to recognize the genre – as "Orly", though it was almost certainly made in Germany. The examples at Audley End were found to include a typical set of dining chairs in William IV style, an ornate washstand and a rococo clock; it was pointed out, however, by the hawk-eyed surveyors that matching tables – swagged, cabriole-legged and claw-footed – and a sofa would originally have formed part of the Orly complement, and it is very satisfying to hear that these missing items were subsequently discovered in a store-cupboard and have now been put back into the doll's house.
>
> Among the wooden pieces there are some good plain mahogany chests of drawers, two three-tier dumb waiters, a folding baize-lined card table and a wooden cage with wire bars occupied by a giant yellow bird borrowed from a Noah's Ark – a charming instance of serendipity, this, in view of Audley End's famous ornithological collection. In the drawing room stands an upright pianoforte with pleated silk panel, tambour lid and the sturdy, tapered, fluted legs of the 1830s – an astonishing number of these pianos in several sizes survive in dozens of period doll's houses. A greater rarity is the beautiful harp, white with pink and blue floral decorations and gold paper trimming, with its eight pegs and strings intact. Another most unusual piece is a round occasional table, four

inches high, supported on a tripod composed of simulated antlers; the table top appears to be boxwood, ornamented with an intaglio design of oak leaves and acorns encircling the figure of a white hound. The fashion for horn furniture in the mid 19th century came from Germany and the Prince Consort bought a set for Osborne in 1846. This well-made miniature probably also came from Germany.

The home-made items show the various needlework skills of the original owners of the house. All the principal rooms have full-length curtains of glowing silk or sprigged chintz, hanging from brass rails and topped with lively festoons or deep pelmets; matching fabrics have been used on the fourpost beds and on a series of upholstered banquettes ranged round the walls of the reception rooms. On close inspection these seats proved to be no more than blocks of rough wood – in some cases cardboard boxes – lightly padded and then covered.

Footstools abound, covered with velvet and embroidered with cut steel beads, and these could well have been made by children. The needlepoint carpets, too, would have presented few difficulties to a patient child, being worked in simple geometric repeat patterns. The most ambitious home-made object in the house is a very pretty cradle; its body and rockers consist of stiff card tightly covered in faced silk of cream, brown and blue stripes.

The residents of this superior dwelling are all jointed wooden Grödnerthal dolls, recognisable as coming from the same source as

The Audley End house is no more than a crudely made toy, but it is filled with interesting miniatures, some home-made, others commercially produced (see page 125).

the celebrated group dressed by the future Queen Victoria and her governess.

As in most doll's houses, the kitchen is perhaps the most engaging of all the rooms, though here the difficulty of identifying and scheduling the individual items of such a hoard of miniature bygones called for exceptional knowledge and expertise.

It was Vivien Greene who identified the kitchen equipment, a task for which she was well qualified as owner of the Rotunda, Oxford, where her unique collection of dolls' houses is kept. Here a house of the same period as Audley End, but on a far less grand scale, can be seen. Stack House (page 102) is a flat-fronted Victorian house with a painted exterior of brick and an imitation painted portico. A painted housekeeper is looking out of a painted window. The house was made in Settle, Yorkshire, but it is not characteristic of real houses in that district, which are made of stone. It remained at the real Stack House with one family for more than a hundred years until it was sold.

All the furniture is original. There are six rooms. On the ground floor are the kitchen, a hall containing a doll and a perambulator, and a well-filled dining room. Upstairs is a music room with a piano and a Walterhausen writing desk. A table is laid for two. A china-headed doll dressed in pink stands by the desk and on the mantelshelf with its paper lace trimming are two clocks, one of which is under glass, and a Victorian ornament, also under glass – these are typical of many made in Britain and Germany at this time. A small central room and a bedroom complete the top floor.

The Rotunda collection contains many more good examples of early 19th-century dolls' houses, among them Whiteway, which dates

The three figures in the library of Whiteway should, rightly, be in the dining room at their Christmas dinner – their positions in the present setting of the house, which, according to Vivien Greene, is Christmas Day at 6 o'clock.

from about 1845. This house was formerly at Saltram House, Plymouth, whose owner, Lord Morley, who died in 1962, gave it to his footman for his small daughter. When the National Trust took over the house the dolls' house had been sold to a local antique dealer, who offered it to the National Trust. The Trust refused it because it was a replica not of Saltram but of an early house which had belonged to the same family; however, it has now been willed back to the Trust.

Vivien Greene describes the interior of the house in detail in her book *Family Dolls' Houses*. The original wall coverings survive except in the hall and linen room. The left-hand bedroom has some original furniture – the bed with its chintz hangings, the matching curtains, and the hand-made carpet of rosebuds on a claret ground. The cast-iron hob grate in the corner is embellished with a fall of flowers and, on each side, with a head of Queen Victoria as a young woman and a crown. It was made by a local blacksmith. In the other bedroom all the furniture except for the dressing stool is original, as is the carpet.

The drawing-room walls are covered in pale blue satin held in place by narrow gilt metal fillets. The pictures have been added, plus a bead chair, a harp, and a "marble" table made by Vivien Greene from dyed and crushed eggshells following a recipe in *The Home Book for Young Ladies*. The curious aquarium, only $1\frac{1}{2}$ in (3.8 cm) high, containing water, water weed, and an arch for goldfish, is at least 120 years old.

Some toys in the schoolroom were added recently, but most are mid-19th century. The maps are neatly mounted and contemporary with the house. The music albums are facsimiles of Victorian songs and there is a case containing ten hand-cut paper butterflies which tremble on minute paper supports in a case less than $1\frac{1}{2}$ in (3.8 cm) long.

The Gothic castle in Vivien Greene's private collection (see page 102).

The books in the library are of carved wood, and each one is different. The globe is a rarity, dated 1851. The fine carpet was already in the room, as was the table, the bible, and most of the furnishings. The tiger- and leopard-skin rugs, one in the hall, one on the landing, are commercially produced. There is no kitchen in this house, but this is not unusual for dolls' houses of the period.

A later dolls' house at the Rotunda, St Faith's Vicarage, is a redbrick Gothic house of eleven rooms. It is lit from the inside, so you can see what is going on. A poignant tale is woven about the doll inhabitants. The vicar and his wife have just received their orphaned niece into their home and, dressed in deep mourning, she sits beneath a daguerreotype of her mother, her black hat beside her on a chair. Her trunk is unpacked in the hall and the vicar is sitting at a roll-top desk writing letters on black-edged notepaper.

Other Rotunda houses of the 19th century are the balustraded house, the Bidden house (which has a door with a stained-glass insert), Queen Victoria's Golden Jubilee house (decorated with flags and bunting to commemorate Victoria's fifty years on the throne), and the Cedars, Woodbridge (a Suffolk house with a long drawing room decorated with gilt pilasters and equipped with 1860–90 furniture).

Not on show at the Rotunda but in the home of Vivien Greene is a 6 ft (1.8 m)-tall Gothic house on a stand (page 101), which opens out to reveal seven rooms in the house itself and six in the towers. The house has a grey-painted composition finish. Its ornate porch is guarded by carved limewood knights which probably date from the early 19th century (there are similar ones in a cabinet at Osborne House, Queen Victoria's house on the Isle of Wight). These knights are miniatures of full-sized statues at Alnwick Castle, medieval home of the Duke of Northumberland, and the dolls' house bears some resemblance to Alnwick. Vivien Greene, though, compares it with the late-18th-century gatehouse at Grimston Garth, Yorkshire.

Stack House, in the collection of the Rotunda, Oxford – its painted front removed to reveal the interior.

Other Victorian Gothic dolls' houses can be seen at the Bethnal Green Museum of Childhood, and at Wallington Hall. Like the others they reflect the Victorian romantic interest in "medieval" history, which also showed itself in the novels of Sir Walter Scott and in the enthusiastic construction of Gothic castles and follies all over the country.

Wallington Hall in Northumberland is a National Trust property which has a remarkable collection of fifteen or so dolls' houses dating from 1845 to 1930, which occupy a large room in the house and overflow into the passage outside.

Most of the dolls' houses, together with their contents, were

This four-roomed house, dated 1886, in the Wallington Hall collection of the National Trust, opens in two halves. The bedroom over the functional-looking kitchen boasts a four-poster bed.

presented to the National Trust in 1973 by the family of Mrs Bridget Angus of Corbridge, who collected them during her lifetime.

The furniture is arranged in the houses by date and quality as far as possible, the oldest in the oldest house and the best in the best house. Some redecoration has been necessary for the interiors, though in old fabrics of the correct date. A six-roomed house, made in about 1840–45, has some particularly good furniture; it also boasts hand-made petit-point carpets throughout and a hand-made embroidered bellpull in one of the rooms.

The star of the collection is undoubtedly the largest – the Hammond house (page 107). This is a mansion of thirty-six rooms, made to order in about 1886, probably by an estate joiner. The house is not remarkable for craftsmanship – it consists simply of a series of boxes connected by service corridors running the length of the house, by two staircases, and by a working lift at one end.

The house was always lit by electricity, which must have been a great innovation when it was first installed, but the wiring has been renewed. Originally water was piped from tanks on the roof to the bathroom, and thence to the scullery below, a delightful piece of realism which has now vanished. The pipes have perished and cannot be replaced without damaging the decorations. All the wallpapers are original and in some cases they are hand-painted, the best example of this being found in the nursery. The carpets are also original, as are most of the furnishings, though some additions were made in the Edwardian period. There is some Walterhausen furniture with gilt decoration, and some metalwork pieces made at Diessen can be seen in the guest bedroom. The set of china in the servants' hall is probably Meissen and the wooden plates in the kitchen are Thuringian. The pink tea set in the breakfast room is of English metal painted by a contemporary hand, as is the unusual dinner service in the dining room, which is painted to look like Meissen. The pieces of milk glass in the house are of Bohemian make. This lavish furnishing demonstrates how easy it was to buy dolls'-house items in the 19th century. They were stocked by almost every toy shop, and if children had the pocket money they could soon have a dolls' house filled with realistic-looking pieces.

There are rooms of all kinds – rooms for servants, for the housekeeper, for children, and for storage; there is a scullery, a drawing room, a governess's bedroom, and a boot room containing an impressive row of bells from which an enclosed staircase rises to the first floor.

The house is filled with china-faced dolls of all kinds, adults and children, and a full complement of domestic staff – maids, nannies, butler, cook, and footmen. The dolls are German, dating from about 1885, and each is dressed in the appropriate costume of the period. It is rare to find so many men dolls in one house – there are several here, two of them in Scottish Highland dress.

Another attractive dolls' house in the Wallington collection is Claremont House, made in 1867 (page 106). The bricks and slates are all painted and the front door has glass panels. This house has its original wallpaper and is furnished with solid wooden pieces in all the six rooms. It has a little front garden with a gate and all the rooms and the hall and the landings can be opened separately. In the kitchen a brick stove stands to one side, giving a middle-European air to the house.

More grand Victorian houses are to be seen at the Bethnal Green Museum of Childhood, in London. Mrs Bryant's Pleasure, a plain, flat-fronted house with a balustrade along the top, was made for Mrs Bryant of Oakenshaw, Surbiton, in the 1860s, its over-sized but well-made furniture especially commissioned. Mrs Bryant was interested in recording the interior decoration of her day and, like it or loathe it (Vivien Greene describes "repellent Japanese jars" and "tremendous half-tester beds"), one cannot but admire the perfect upholstering of

Nine of the thirty-six well-filled rooms of the Hammond house, the largest in Wallington Hall's collection.

the armchairs and the finish of the tables and dining-room chairs. We must also admire Mrs Bryant's handiwork in the curtains and carpets.

Dingley Hall, also at Bethnal Green, was made in 1874 and is named after a house near Market Harborough. It was made for two boys, Isaac and Laurence Currie, which alone is unusual – boys seem rarely to have been interested in dolls' houses. Laurence, who was fourteen when the house was made, had begun to collect miniatures as a small child and he added to his collection all his adult life, picking up items on his frequent travels abroad and bringing them home for the house. Some of the furniture was quite expensive; £25 for a Venetian glass chandelier purchased by B. W. Currie in 1882 seems wildly extravagant. The house, which is very large and dominated by its velvet-curtained chapel, is full of masculine detail, such as several dolls dressed as Hussars and, on the walls, weapons, shields holding trophies, and a stag's head.

Miss Miles' House, made by Miss Amy Miles in the 1890s, is a

Claremont House (RIGHT) *has its name on the front and its date (1867) under the front gate. The house is equipped throughout with solidly made wooden furniture.*

OPPOSITE: *some of the electrically lit and fully furnished rooms of the Hammond house.*

squarish house with an additional section at the side. Vivien Greene believes it to be a commercially made dolls' house to which extra rooms were added. It is furnished in an up-to-the-minute manner, with a shower, a geyser to warm the bathroom water, a telephone in the billiards room, a carpet sweeper in the lumber room and a tap at the kitchen sink. Old photographs show that from the lumber room on the top floor a ladder led to a penthouse studio, but the studio is no longer there. The lumber room on the ground floor contains, rather unexpectedly, a bathchair. The house is well populated with dolls. The servants are correctly dressed, the ladies are in fashionable clothes, and the men are very splendid, dressed in tweeds, with handsome moustaches.

Dolls' houses have often been stripped of their furniture before being sold, the pieces disposed of in lots to make more profit, a reprehensible practice which poses a problem for restorers. The choice is between making do with an empty house, filling it with reproduction furniture, or equipping it with authentic period furniture. There is a sharp division of opinion on the subject. In England the purists are led by Faith Eaton, who has furnished the houses in her private collection with authentic furniture of the period or not at all. Furnishing with authentic pieces is hard to achieve not only because of the prohibitive prices of collectors' items but because of the time it takes to search them out. Faith Eaton would rather have a house without any wallpaper or floor covering than use modern substitutes. To get authentic wall

An English neo-classical dolls' house of about 1810, from the collection at the Bethnal Green Museum of Childhood.

coverings she sometimes uses endpapers from old books or puts in genuine old full-sized wallpaper, hiding its flowers or patterns with pictures or ornaments. After all, many dolls'-house owners in the past had to do the same thing, since especially made smallscale dolls'-house papers are a recent innovation.

Floor coverings were never plentiful in older full-sized houses, so floor boards can be left uncovered or carpeted with old fabric or papers. It is still possible occasionally to find old fabric for re-upholstery. Vivien Greene describes how she went to a sale of effects of an old house which was being demolished and spotted a long length of crimson silk brocade from the walls lying on the ground. She obtained a foot or two and used it to cover the dolls'-house chairs in Cane End house in the Rotunda.

Many of Faith Eaton's dolls' houses have come to her in a state of complete ruin. Her oldest house, Yoakley Lodge, was bought as little more than a pile of wood, treated with preservative to keep out the worms. She skillfully put the house together and it is now the most interesting in her collection. Dated 1852, Yoakley Lodge was made for a little girl named Emma Bennet by her godfather's carpenter and given to her as a seventh birthday present. Emma Bennet's daughter, as an old lady, remembered being told how the key to the dolls'-house door had been placed under her mother's plate at breakfast time so that she would have the thrill of discovering what it unlocked. The daughter also remembered the house as it was when it was fully furnished, though Faith Eaton acquired it with little of the original furniture and is having difficulty in finding the right period pieces for it. The dolls are original, although she has mended and re-dressed them, using old fabrics.

Perhaps the most interesting room in Yoakley Lodge is the kitchen, which has a fine fireplace with its old range and a wooden dresser of the kind commonly found in kitchens of the 1850s. Kitchen accessories include a metal box in which tallow candles were kept to keep them safe from hungry rats and mice, a metal plate warmer which stood in front of the open fire, and the heavy pans and entrée dishes which were a necessity in Victorian days.

Faith Eaton is an expert on English costume, with a sharp eye for the hierarchy of "below stairs", so the servants are all accurately dressed in period style. The cook wears a print dress and cap and an apron without a bib. The maid is also in a print dress. It was not until later in the 19th century that parlour maids were put into black for the afternoons. Before that, as they were not seen above stairs, it did not matter much what they wore. Footmen and butlers were always dressed in livery. Cook and maid are talking to the groom, whose vertically striped waistcoat identifies him as an outside servant.

A favourite dolls' house, which was a gift to Faith Eaton, is Contented Cot, a charming little wooden house made in 1886 by Henry Hall, a master mariner of Brixham, Devon, for his small daughter (whose birth announcement was found pasted inside the roof). The

The delightful balconied front of Contented Cot, with a doll watching the world outside from an upstairs window.

house is well made, with plenty of architectural detail, windows that open and shut, and a door with a knocker and fanlight. The master mariner also made all the sturdy furniture for the house.

Hartley Hall, a much grander commercially made house of the period (1880), has numerous large windows and detailed carving on the cornice, which is repeated in bands under the windows. These are remarkable in a dolls' house, reminding one of the Bel Air house (page 116) and also of a house sold in London recently by Sotheby's (page 112), which was described as "Iberian *c.*1860". This rarity was on three floors, with eight French windows opening on to galleried balconies. Each window had a carved motif above and was flanked by gadrooned panels (that is, decorative patterns formed of a series of convex ridges). Inside were eight rooms and a hall.

There are dozens more 19th-century English dolls' houses in museums and private collections up and down the country. Some, though, are in museums which rarely show them to the public. The Wythenshaw collection, Manchester, for example, has an early-19th-century travelling dolls' house with handles and a castellated top and a large cupboard-type house of four rooms with papered walls and two

A slightly dissolute-looking Victorian family in their cluttered drawing room – one of the rooms in a Victorian dolls' house in the Bethnal Green Museum of Childhood.

drawers in the base dated 1831, both of which were sighted recently at an exhibition. Wythenshaw also has a large Georgian-style painted wooden house of four rooms. Another Wythenshaw treasure which has not been seen for some years but has been described by Vivien Greene is a dolls' house with eight rooms and a staircase, dated 1830–40. An unusual feature, and one which many dolls'-house enthusiasts would like to see, is the schoolroom, complete with desks, blackboard, and *trompe-l'œil* paintings of little slates bearing the names of the students.

AMERICAN DOLLS' HOUSES

There was no mass production of dolls' houses in America in the first part of the century, so the few examples that survive from this period are all hand made. One early and distinguished craftsman was the Rev. Philip Milledoler Brett, who spent the years from 1838 to 1840 building a dolls' house which is one of the twelve houses now preserved in the museum of the City of New York. The toy gallery of this museum has recently been re-designed and during the two years of reconstruction the dolls' houses were cleaned, repaired, and re-wired. The exterior of the Brett house is not as elaborate as some of the later American houses.

Sunburst ornaments on the front doors of (BELOW) *a flat-fronted early-20th-century G. & J. Lines house and* (BOTTOM RIGHT) *a late-19th-century Victorian house.*

BOTTOM LEFT: *the intricate and airy exterior of Hartley Hall.*

The centre is two-storied and the side wings one-storied, an arrangement quite unlike that of English houses of the same period. The house is surrounded by a walled garden in which grandmother and grandfather are having tea. At the back is a staircase hall lit by two windows with arched fanlights and there is a cellar for storage. A portrait of the Rev. Brett hangs in the drawing room, which has two French windows.

Most of the furnishings are contemporary with the house but some pieces, such as the books and silver, are earlier. Among the books are a 1786 edition of Robert Burns' poems measuring $1\frac{1}{4}$ ins (3 cm) $\times \frac{3}{4}$ in (1.9 cm), a Lilliputian folio edition of *A Description of England*, and an English dictionary. A copy of Gray's *Elegy* and a bible printed in 1780 are seen on a slant-topped four-shelf bookstand in the drawing room,

This house, catalogued as "Iberian, c.1860" when it was auctioned, bears a resemblance to Hartley Hall (page 111).

where there is also a music stand with music on it, a harp, and an inlaid mandolin. The silver items include a Monteith bowl from London (1775–6), a French wine cooler dated about 1800, and a caudle cup of 1775 (a caudle was a warm drink of wine and eggs given to invalids and women in childbed).

Another superior early house in the same museum is the Shelton Taylor house, dated 1835 and described as having Biedermeier interiors (see pages 120–21 for a definition of this term).

In 1975 Mrs Flora Gill Jacobs opened her Washington Dolls' House and Toy Museum, which represents nearly forty years of collecting and includes many excellent houses as well as authentically furnished shops, schools, and churches and toys and games. One of her early acquisitions was a model of a South Jersey house of about 1850 with a sandpaper-textured exterior, a great many pedimented windows, a convex mansard roof, and eight rooms. She also has a splendid mid-19th-century New York town house, said to have been made for the Tiffany family, that in its elaboration foreshadows the confections of thirty years later.

The Warren house (page 117) at the Essex Institute, Salem, Mass. is a mid-19th-century house of some importance. It was commissioned by Mrs J. Mason Warren (*née* Annie Crowninshield) for her four daughters in 1852 and made by a cabinet maker to her plan. It is a tall house, 6 ft (1.8 m) high, slightly reminiscent of a Nuremberg house, with a fairly plain exterior. A great deal of loving care was lavished on the contents – most of the linen is monogrammed. Mrs Warren made the imitation Aubusson drawing-room carpet with its design of roses and leaves on a white ground, and probably much else besides. Flora Gill Jacobs writes:

> Mrs C. H. Gibson, one of Mrs Warren's daughters, who presented the doll house to the Institute in 1925, took the trouble to submit with it a detailed history ... inside the tall desk in the dining room, for instance, is a "walnut shell with white gloves enclosed which was handed to Mrs Warren at her engagement dinner".
>
> The most historically interesting piece is also in the dining room. The mahogany drop-leaf dinner table is said to have been captured from a British ship in the War of 1812 by the Crownin-shield privateer ship, *America*. The former was all fitted with furniture, brocades and even toys for a family going to India, and this little table was going to India.
>
> The library is copied from the one in the Warren house at 2 Park Street, Boston, which was torn down about 1876.... Tall oak bookcases on either side of the fireplace reaching nearly to the ceiling, with marble busts on top. Red silk curtains cover the front, as there were not enough books to fill them. A red velvet valance with gold fringe hung from the mantel, over which was a mirror with a beautiful carved gold frame.... In front of the fireplace stood a small chess table carved in black and white ivory with legs like a stag's antlers and on it a little green box containing the chessmen no larger than a grain of rice.

The stag's-antler table sounds very much like the one at Audley End, and was doubtless imported.

Massachusetts can also boast the famous Chamberlain dolls' house at Wenham, built in 1884 by Benjamin H. Chamberlain, a silversmith of Salem, as a Christmas present for his two daughters, Mamie and Millie, whose names are inscribed on a silver name-plate on the front door. Naturally enough, Benjamin Chamberlain made many silver items for the house, including a lovely tea set, and he also made and decorated most of the furniture. This eight-roomed house, with gables, a turret room, and a porch, is a much more elaborate and decorative structure than the Warren house. Chamberlain made the gilded railings on the cupola, the central bay, and the kitchen wing and the lovely carving on the stained-wood exterior. His wife is said to have made the curtains, linens, and doll clothes, staying up late on Christmas Eve to finish them. The detail is remarkable: an outlet above the stove in the kitchen leads to a chimney with a lid, there is a built-in dresser with a tap, the windows in the cupola are glazed red, the rooms behind the attic dormers are furnished, and a shell collection is displayed in the parlour.

The Hayes house, in the Rutherford B. Hayes library, Fremont, Ohio, is an equally fanciful creation. Made in 1878 for Fanny Hayes, daughter of the then President, the house was built by carpenter and builder George C. Brown. It has three storeys, a centre turret, bays on three sides, and huge stair halls.

The Smithsonian Institute, Washington D.C. has another ornate house with balustrades, a turret, gables, bay windows, and fretwork imitation wrought iron. Sweeping flights of exterior steps are topped by tall gas lamps and the end result looks for all the world like a setting for one of those film musicals about turn-of-the-century family life in Philadelphia.

One of the most imposing houses in the Washington Dolls' House and Toy Museum comes from Puebla, Mexico. Although its history can be traced back only as far as 1922 when it changed ownership, it is thought to have been built in about 1890 by a Mexican craftsman. It reflects the French architectural influence which prevailed in full-sized houses after Napoleon III's attempt to set up a puppet Mexican Empire under Maximilian. It is about 6 ft (1.8 m) high and over 5 ft (1.5 m) wide and has a great many rooms behind its pillared facade, including a kitchen with a yellow Mexican "tile" oven on a wall filled with local pottery. It also has a chapel with a gilded altar and other typical Mexican gold ornamentation. There is a wrought-iron cupola on the top and floors are reached either by the glass-encased elevator or by the outside staircase through whose well the elevator rises. On the roof garden there are potted plants, a dovecote with six doves, and a gilded birdcage. A pipe leads from a tin water tower to a tiled sink on the roof garden, which probably once held a menagerie. The many windows, towers, and columns hint at the luxury of the rooms inside.

A recent acquisition of the Washington Dolls' House and Toy

Museum is the Bel Air (Maryland) house, another delightful icing-sugar confection made for five little girls of the Dibb family in 1885. On the roof is a "captain's walk" – a path for wives to pace while waiting for seafaring husbands to return.

For each of these masterpieces in wood and metal, there were hundreds of unexceptional two-up, two-down boxes made by American fathers for their children, by the children themselves, or by manufacturers, who had begun to market their wares well before the end of the century. The firm of Rufus Bliss was established as early as 1832, Schoenhut in 1872, and Converse before 1883, though the typical

The Chamberlain house at Wenham, Massachusetts, offers a glimpse of the dining-room table through its right-hand ground-floor window.

lithograph-on-paper houses for which they were famous became widespread only at the beginning of the next century.

PAPER DOLLS' HOUSES

The late 19th century also saw the arrival of dolls' houses made of cardboard. Paper dolls' houses had been known before this in France and Germany as well as the United States. In the 1830s German firms were printing designs that could be cut out and stuck together to make houses. In France, cut-out paper dolls'-house books were popular, but three-dimensional cardboard dolls' houses were something of a novelty. A charming cardboard cottage was invented in 1868 by Mrs Russell and manufactured by G. W. Cottrell of Boston; the front had shutters that opened to reveal rooms within. The firm of McLoughlin listed in their 1875–6 catalogue a folding dolls' house consisting of two pieces of printed card which slotted together to form a four-room apartment – an excellent idea for an inexpensive, storable toy. According to McLoughlin's catalogue: "The house folds down to the above size [13 in (33 cm) × 13 in (33 cm) × 13 in (33 cm)]. It makes four rooms, parlor, dining room, bed-room and kitchen, each 13 in square, without roof, parted off by partitions 13 in high. It is designed to be played with on a table. A number of little girls may thus get round it to the very best advantage. It is made of stout binder's board covered with coloured designs representing the carpets, walls, windows, mantels etc as seen in a house. It is designed to be furnished with paper or other small furniture and to be occupied by paper or other small dolls."

OPPOSITE: *the eight rooms and staircase hall of the Warren house.*

The ornate Bel Air house (BELOW) *is in the same collection, in the Washington Dolls' House and Toy Museum, as the simple bungalow* (BELOW RIGHT) *made by the American firm of Converse towards the end of the 19th century. The details were colour-printed on to the wooden structure.*

There were other types of folding houses – the Spielzeugmuseum, Nuremberg, has a book dated 1880, *The Doll's House, a Festival Gift for Good Girls*, in which a whole series of rooms could be opened out and seen at the same time, the floors folding forward.

The English Toy Company, set up in 1889 to compete with the German market, distributed the components for its toys to outworkers, who assembled them in their homes. "The toy that the Company particularly prides itself upon bears the attractive name of Miss Dollie Daisie Dimple," reported *Tinsley's Magazine*. "This young lady is provided with an elegant detached villa, tastefully furnished and with all kinds of necessaries and luxuries."

A sketch showed a family of three ladies and two small boys working at a round table, houses stacked up nearby. The luxurious items meant to gladden Dollie Daisie Dimple's heart were "distributed to the home-workers. These are mostly children, though among them are a considerable number of adults, some of the most competent of whom are able to earn as much as 17 shillings a week. The youngsters in their cottage homes find very congenial employment in building up doll's houses and the English Toy Company does them good service in enabling them to earn a few shillings weekly, and at the same time, keeping them out of mischief."

Miss Dollie Daisie Dimple was provided with a house, known as Dimple Villa. It had "imitation Red Brick and Stone Facings, Bay Windows, Green Venetian Blinds, Bright Colours &c. A practical two-roomed house to put furniture in. The interior decorations are all in the modern style, Dados, Bright Wallpapers &c. Can be taken to pieces and packed flat for transit or storage and can be rebuilt in a few seconds. This toy is sure to be a favorite with little girls, and all old friends of DOLLIE DAISIE DIMPLE. It is quite a large Doll's House, and takes the place of a Doll's House usually costing ten times the money. Price ONE SHILLING Complete".

MINIATURES

Nineteenth-century miniatures, although expensive, are still obtainable by collectors, mainly because they were produced in such large quantities. France, Britain, and Germany were all making furniture and exporting it (Germany in greater quantities than France or Britain), so dolls' houses of this period tend to be furnished in a mixture of national styles which could never have been found in real houses. The overcrowding of rooms seems to have been a universal characteristic of Victorian interior decoration and one which manufacturers were not slow to exploit.

The variety of items produced is amazing. Kettles, tea services, clocks, sewing boxes, mirrors, cutlery, lamps, birdcages, fireplaces and fire irons, all made in every kind of material, flowed from factories to toyshops, where they were sold for sums well within the reach of middle-class children.

OPPOSITE: (TOP LEFT) *fish, a joint of meat, and fruit – all made in Germany from gutta-percha;* (TOP RIGHT) *bathroom and toilet furniture, including a WC, a commode, a washbasin, and a shower – both sets from Vivien Greene's collection; and* (BOTTOM) *a blue-and-white dinner service made in Germany.*

119

German dolls'-house furniture is to be seen in most of the 19th-century interiors shown in this book, alongside home-made and indigenous products. Germany had a long tradition of toymaking and its miniatures had found their way all over the world by the end of the century. German toy manufacturers were well organized – their products were cheap and well marketed.

Different towns and districts tended to concentrate on one type of miniature, so we find ivory, bone, and wood carvings from Berchtesgaden, wooden jointed dolls'-house dolls from Grödnertal, and tin furniture from Nuremberg and Württemberg. The orange-painted "Orly" furniture in the Audley End house is an example of this type of tinware, but picture frames, cooking utensils, fireplaces, clocks, candlesticks and other small and desirable items were also made. Metal filigree work was another German speciality and the page from the toy manufacturer's catalogue (shown on page 125) illustrates the remarkably high standard of workmanship that was achieved. Diessen was the centre for this and remained so until the 1920s. Thuringia was known both for its glassware and for its pottery; Walterhausen was famous for its wooden furniture.

The term "Walterhausen" is used in this book to describe a particular type of wooden dolls'-house furniture which was made in different sizes and patterns for most of the century. It is easily recognizable, for it is strongly made in imitation ebony and gold or in rosewood and gold. It is also called "Biedermeier" or "Dolls'-house Duncan Phyfe", after a well-known American furniture maker. Constance Eileen King, in *The Collector's History of Dolls' Houses*, gives this account of it:

Dolls'-house accessories like these are now much sought-after collectors' items – (BELOW) *a punch set of six glasses in a stand;* (BOTTOM) *a coffee set in its original box (the message inside reads, "A. Curtis, the gift of her brother, John, on her fifth birthday, August 22nd 1845");* *and* (BOTTOM RIGHT) *early-19th-century miniature birdcages, only about 4½ in (11.5 cm) high.*

This furniture is sometimes claimed to date from the 1830s as its basic style is in sympathy with that period. In general, however, the pieces, now generally believed to have originated in Walterhausen, are made in the styles of the 1860s and 1870s, and it seems more than likely that they were in fact the first products of Schneegass, established in 1845. . . . The Biedermeier style, upon which many of the earlier designs are based, was itself very much the expression of German middle-class taste, and it was for the children of such homes that the miniatures were intended.

The Biedermeier style had originated in Austria and Germany during the years 1815–48. The word was coined from the German words *bieder*, meaning plain or unpretentious, and *meier*, a common German surname. It was first used, in a derogatory sense, to mean lack of pretension and artistic worth, but the simple style was refreshing after the opulence of French Empire furniture and its graceful lines are pleasing to modern taste.

To sum up, the dolls'-house furniture is correctly called "Walterhausen" while "Biedermeier" and "Duncan Phyfe" describe the design styles on which it is based.

Another type of dolls'-house furniture is the German lithographed paper-on-wood pieces in bright colours which came to the fore towards the end of the century. Brash and cheerful, they must have been much loved by children.

In Britain, as in Germany, different types of furniture were made in different places. Whitby was famed for its jetware; Tunbridge Wells for its pretty inlaid miniature furniture; Birmingham for brass and copper kettles, jugs, kitchen utensils, and fenders. London and Birmingham were tin and pewter toy centres, producing a large number of cast-metal tea, coffee, and dinner sets – *Chamber's Journal* reported in 1877 that one girl in a factory could cast 2,500 small tea cups in a day.

French 19th-century gilded metal "Louis XV" miniature furniture – an open armchair, a side table, and a chaise longue.

OPPOSITE: *this splendid floral furniture* (TOP LEFT) *is of wood covered with lithographed paper. The household utensils* (BOTTOM LEFT) – *covered cooking dishes, a grater, a strainer or sieve, and a bedwarmer – are English, made of pewter and tin.*

A group of furniture from Audley End (ABOVE) *includes an Orly clock, a dining chair, and a table with antler legs.*

English dolls'-house lighting (RIGHT) – *a candlestick, a conical storm lantern, a glass-panelled gas lantern, and an oil lamp.*

Staffordshire potters had always produced a small amount of miniature ware – Wedgwood items are to be found in 18th-century dolls' houses and some small Wedgwood pieces were still made in the 19th century. Rockingham, Whieldon, Leeds, and Bow are all known to have produced small tea and dinner services, although they were not necessarily small enough, or intended, for dolls' houses. However, there was little incentive for English potters to compete with the cheaper German products.

Fashions came and went. Fretwork became popular towards the end of the century – there are examples in the Audley End house (presumably added at a later date) and in the Hammond house. In the United States, "Scroll Saw" designs were printed not only for furniture but for complete houses. Metal chairs and tables are found in later-19th-century houses alongside wooden ones.

Late-19th-century Walterhausen furniture (RIGHT, TOP) in wood with gilt decoration – two dressing tables complete with mirrors and a glass-fronted bookcase.

A set of graceful porcelain and bronze late-19th-century furniture (RIGHT), decorated with scenes of lovers in country settings.

Any conveniently small household objects were also pressed into use as dolls'-house furnishings, such as pincushions in the shape of stools (Denton Welch, writing about restoring dolls' houses, says, "I found a little emery needle cushion in the form of a tiny stool"), seaside souvenirs intended as mantelshelf ornaments, or small pieces of ivory from India. Baxter prints, sold on packets of needles, made excellent pictures when they were framed. Every kind of material was used – wood, tin, pewter, pottery, wire, beads, and bone (as a substitute for ivory).

Mothers, nannies, or children, using instructional books as guides, made bed covers, curtains, cushions, and carpets. They could also make chairs out of pin-and-thread, quill, and beadwork and cupboards, beds, and tables from cardboard, so that a miniature home could be comfortably arranged in no time.

America had imported toys from Europe in the 18th century but American-made pewter and tin toys were available at an early date. Philadelphia was a centre of manufacture for these and other metal items, the firm of Francis, Field and Francis reproducing chairs, tables, clocks, and other household pieces as early as 1853. Another firm made imitation rosewood furniture with velvet upholstery in tin, which must have taken some doing.

J. and S. Stevens Company of Cromwell, Connecticut, made iron

Intricately detailed filigree pieces from a catalogue of dolls'-house tableware.

125

Fretwork furniture of the 19th century – three chairs and a settee (lacking an arm rail).

toys, among them "wash stands, fruit baskets, cook stoves, laundry stoves, Franklin stoves, coal hods with shovels . . .'.

Rare American tin toys can be seen in the 19th-century New Hampshire house at the Washington Doll's House and Toy Museum.

We must not forget dolls'-house food, that essential for the well-equipped kitchen. Nineteeth-century food was often made of gutta percha, a gummy material which has not lasted well, but food made of pottery and plaster has a long life, and little dishes of oysters, cauliflower, or cakes, looking as good as new, are still occasionally to be found. Joints of meat, in the early 19th century made in wood to hang from bottlejacks, were later reproduced in the same style in plaster and gutta percha.

THE 20TH CENTURY

The two great dolls' houses of the 20th century, Queen Mary's dolls' house and Titania's Palace, are in the baby-house tradition, filled with craftsman-made miniatures. But there are, of course, many humbler houses that reflect the life style and architecture of ordinary homes more closely than these two extravagant flights of fancy.

Some contained "mod cons" never dreamed of in the past, like electric light, bathrooms with working plumbing, and even, in one instance, gas. Many were made by devoted relatives from patterns published in magazines. But the 20th century has, on the whole, been the age of the smaller manufactured dolls' house, like the pretty German house (below), dated 1920, with its mansard roof and balconies, measuring a convenient 23 in (58 cm) × 25½ in (65 cm) × 16 in (41 cm). This is much lighter in style than earlier houses like that on page 128, which is in the Spielzeugmuseum, Nuremberg, and is dated 1910. This is a craftsman-made house with coffered ceilings, solid wood

The ornate front of this German dolls' house (BELOW LEFT) of about 1920 conceals a dining room, a small kitchen, a bathroom, a large sitting room, and an attic room.

A 20th-century French house (BELOW) in the Musée des Arts Décoratifs, Paris, with a delightful steepled tower and dainty porch.

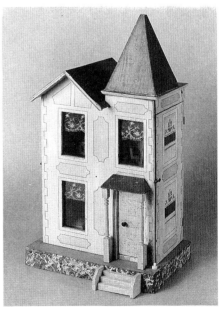

furniture, marquetry floors, and a laundry room upstairs rather like those in the old Dutch baby houses. Another German house of 1910, which appeared at auction recently, has four rooms and two halls and is enlivened with floral wallpapers, thin curtains, and white paint. This house, which must surely be home-made, is quite large, measuring 34 in (86 cm) × 47 in (120 cm) × 16½ in (42 cm).

To move further north, the Nordiska Museet, Stockholm, has two modern houses. One is dated 1900–05, the other – a copy of Hersbyholm Manor at Lidingo, Stockholm – is dated 1925. It was made by a local carpenter and its clean lines and austere but beautifully proportioned frontage are firmly in the Scandinavian idiom. A couple is sitting at a tea table in a room which also contains a large Christmas tree surrounded by wrapped gifts, a piano, two bookcases, and a little tea trolley on wheels. The walls are plain, the lighting and the curtains modern. It is a comfortably uncluttered room, providing a great contrast to rooms of thirty years before.

The Museovirasti, Helsinki, Finland, has a 1930 cabinet dolls' house of six rooms which once belonged to Birgitta and Kati Lojander.

The well-detailed interior of the 1910 German house at Nuremberg (BELOW).

Hersbyholm Manor in miniature (RIGHT, TOP) *and* (BOTTOM RIGHT) *ready for Christmas in the sitting room with its 1920s modernistic furniture.*

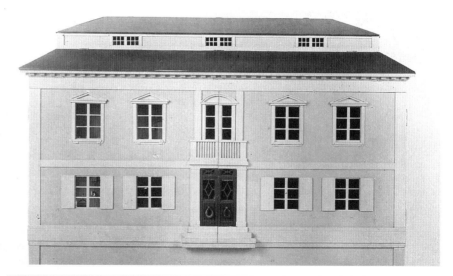

On the ground floor is a sitting room with very modern white furniture. Next to it is an open-plan kitchen with a staircase rising from it. The cooking stove is placed, rather unsuitably, under the staircase and there is another oddity in the kitchen – a sort of bathroom cubicle containing a modern toilet, bath, and basin. Above this room is a nursery and a dining room; on the top floor there is a study and a bedroom furnished with fretwork furniture.

Some delightful 20th-century dolls' houses come from Japan, but little is known about them in the West. Mrs F. Nevill Jackson, in *Toys of Other Days*, says of one Japanese dolls' house: "Madame Chrysanthemum has the most charmingly furnished house in all doll-land and her equipment is complete, even to a two-inch lacquer box with dollie's writing-brush, Indian ink tablet, palette, and water-bottle, lest she should wish to write a letter". Mrs Jackson describes elsewhere how Japanese dolls' houses are connected with an annual doll festival, celebrated on 3 March, during which parents pray for the happiness of their daughters. Dolls and their equipment are arranged on shelves draped with red cloths. In the place of honour on the top shelf sit a court noble and his lady. On the shelves below are courtiers, musicians, and servants and, on the bottom shelf, miniature furnishings in black lacquer – tiny chests of drawers, mirrors, writing tables, and boxes – and cakes made of rice or beans.

The two tiny Japanese dolls' houses in Faith Eaton's collection may, in fact, belong to the 19th century rather than the 20th. One is about 6 in (15 cm) high, the other 9 in (23 cm). They are made of wood

The impeccably furnished dolls' house that once belonged to the Logander sisters.

and bamboo and their finish is impeccable, with fine straw inlays, sliding screen doors, and mesh windows. A third Japanese house, belonging to Mrs Zandra Constable of Edinburgh, is similar in style, with straw inlay and a liberal use of bamboo and wood. It is on two floors.

Accompanying Faith Eaton's Japanese houses is an extraordinary and fascinating set of wooden furniture (page 145). The pieces fit so precisely into their box that a plan of their arrangement is necessary as a guide to replace them once they have been taken out. Only about 2 in (5 cm) high, they are exquisitely made. The tiny metal tea bowls stack into neat piles which fit into the central section of the cupboard on the right. Then the inlaid wooden front slides into place to keep the contents safe. At the front is a mirror and a set of wooden cooking implements about $\frac{1}{2}$ in (1.25 cm) high. At the back of the group is a desk with a stool, inside which nests another stool. On the left are two chests of drawers, one patterned with a mosaic of tiny pieces of differently coloured woods.

The wooden Russian house (page 145), from the collection of Mrs Lorna Gandolfo, is also quite small, measuring about 18 in (45 cm) high. Made in traditional country style with hand-painted decoration, it could date from any period between about 1780 and 1934. The doll fits into the box on which it now stands. It came from Vyatka, now Kirov in Siberia, perhaps brought out of Russia at the time of the Russian Revolution.

AMERICAN DOLLS' HOUSES

After the turn of the century, the toy-manufacturing industry in America became well established. Prominent among the manufacturers was the firm of Rufus Bliss, which by 1907 was producing an extensive line of stables, stores, cabins, and so on, as well as dolls' houses.

OPPOSITE: *the Rufus Bliss manufacturing company of Pawtucket, Rhode Island, was famous for its colourfully decorated dolls' houses, made of wood covered with lithographed paper. A house identical to this, described as "late 19th century", was sold by Sotheby's, New York, in April 1985, for $1,210 (£950).*

*The pretty American Schoenhut bungalow of about 1917 (*RIGHT*) carries much more architectural detail than the bungalow made by the rival firm of Converse shown on page 116.*

Although the houses were "made in American designs to suit the tastes of American children", some were exported to Britain. Bliss houses were richly decorated, in late-20th-century style, and embellished with gables, dormers, porches, balconies, and turned wooden pillars. Some had isinglass windows and lace curtains; others had lithographed windows. The houses were quite compact, only about 25 in (64 cm) to 26 in (66 cm) high, and were suited, therefore, to small modern homes. Some could be folded flat – they were made of heavy board hinged with cloth.

Bliss also made lithographed paper-on-wood dolls' houses. They were advertised as being "true to nature" and, although they scarcely justify this description, they were certainly attractive, with their brightly coloured balconies and "tiled" roofs and porches. The style was imitated everywhere, in France and other European countries as well as by rival United States manufacturers such as Schoenhut and Converse. Later some houses were lithographed directly on to wood.

The firm of Schoenhut was founded in Philadelphia in 1872 by Albert Schoenhut, who had emigrated there from Germany. He produced "very authentic, artistic, high class doll houses and bungalows in new styles of modern architecture". The bungalows were (and still are, for they have retained their bright colours) very pretty, featuring turned balustrades on the porches, net curtains at the windows, and (a novel touch) lithographed doorways on the walls showing a perspective view of another room beyond. Bungalows had from one to four rooms and side openings so as not to spoil the look of the fronts. They usually rested on a stone-look base. Houses like this were produced until 1927.

The firm of Converse was established in 1878, initially making boxes but soon moving into dolls' houses. Converse made lithograph-on-wood bungalows, with fairly primitive designs on them, almost without change until 1926.

One early-20th-century hand-made model typical of its period is the Stettheimer house in the Museum of the City of New York. It was made by Carrie Stettheimer in 1923, out of wooden packing cases and she decorated the rooms herself. Though the house cannot be described as a fine piece of work, it is interesting and unusual because of the artistic skill of the maker.

The outside of the house is unremarkable but the inside is furnished in Carrie Stettheimer's idiosyncratic style. There are rooms on all sides and at the centre of the front of the house is an entrance hall with a formal perspective garden which disappears into the distance in the manner of the gardens in Dutch 18th-century houses. On the left is a blue and white kitchen, on the right a library-cum-games room, with a Chinese-type hanging lantern, red furniture, spindly chairs and some books, one of them by Henri Waste, the curious pseudonym adopted by Carrie's novelist sister. Upstairs is a linen room in black and white with black lace edging, a nursery with its own dolls' house and brightly painted wallpaper, and the master bedroom with green gilded furniture and pink walls. Other rooms include a butler's pantry, servants' room, dining room, parlor, children's rooms, and the art room – which contains miniature paintings by famous American artists of the 1920s. The house and its colour schemes are not to everyone's taste but the house does depict the life style of a wealthy, cultured family of the era.

Another famous modern American dolls' house (in the Museum of Science and Industry, Chicago) depicts the fantasy world of sixty years ago in a rich mixture of myth, legend, fairy tale, and Hollywood glitz. Colleen Moore's fairy-tale castle was made, in copper and aluminium, by her father in collaboration with a film-set designer. Begun in 1928, the castle is "Early Faery" in period, the 1920s being rather preoccupied with the possible existence of fairies at the bottom of the garden. (Sir Nevile Wilkinson, creator of Titania's Palace in England a few years before, had also indulged in whimsical fancies of this kind.)

The castle is 12 ft (3.7 m) high, with battlements, turrets, and pinnacled towers. It has eleven rooms filled with expensive, glittering treasures, some of which were especially made for Colleen. There are stained-glass windows illustrating fairy tales, paintings of characters from children's books, and, in the drawing room, a chandelier made from diamonds, emeralds, and pearls.

The dining room represents the Great Dining Hall of King Arthur and his Knights. It contains a semi-circular table around which are tall shield-backed chairs bearing the occupants' coats of arms. The table service is made of gold, the forks each marked with a monogram almost too small to see with the naked eye. On the stone walls are tapestries telling the life story of Sir Galahad. The library contains miniature books by American authors. The great hall has a vaulted ceiling. The garden (in which a nightingale sings) has gold and silver trees, splashing fountains, and a weeping-willow tree that really weeps. Cinderella's silver coach, drawn by four silver horses, waits outside and Santa Claus is perched on the castle walls.. The steeple bells chime every five minutes and, in the chapel, a cherub-infested organ plays suitable music from the hundred keys.

It is an amazing creation and one wonders what Sara Ploos Van Amstel would have made of it all. She would, perhaps, have approved of the gold monogrammed dinner service and the silver trees.

ENGLISH DOLLS' HOUSES

Most early-20th-century English houses made by craftsmen were still rooted in the past, their exteriors those of typically substantial late-Victorian villas. Number 3 Devonshire Villas, in the Bethnal Green Museum of Childhood, dated about the turn of the century, takes its name from a house in Kilburn High Road, London, in which Mr Samuel Loebe lived with his family in 1900. It is to some extent a replica of the family house and the furniture, too, may have been copied from that in the real house. Samuel Loebe made the dolls' house for his daughter. It contains a bedroom, a nursery, a small bathroom, an ornate dining room, a sitting room, a kitchen, and a staircase.

The bedroom is particularly fine. Its white-painted suite is in the style of the 1880s, and there is a lot of detail – ornaments on the chest at the foot of the bed, brushes, bowls, and toilet articles on the dressing table, lace antimacassars on the backs of the chair and chaise longue, two Dutch scenes in blue and white, and white china on the wash stand. There are three electric lights, with beaded shades, even though there are also two candlesticks in the room – the Loebes were clearly not putting all their trust in the new-fangled electricity.

The sitting room is modern in feeling; the overmantel is painted

The sitting room of 3 Devonshire Villas, with an overcrowded nursery and small bathroom above.

Two small lithographed paper-on-wood early-20th-century houses (LEFT) *from the Precinct Toy Collection, Sandwich, and* (BELOW) *the dining room of a 1908 house (see page 136) in the same collection.*

white and the stuffed easy chair and sofa, of around 1910, are comfortably un-Victorian. There is a black baby grand piano in the corner and a few landscapes on the wall. Typical of the period are the high picture rail, the standard and side lights with their silk shades, and the decorative bead curtain that is used to cover the door to the first-floor conservatory.

The nursery contains five babies – they and a cat are the only inhabitants of this dolls' house. One child is in a modern high chair, the other in a baby walker rather like those in the Nuremberg houses of nearly 300 years before.

Items typical of the time can be seen thoughout the house – a wall telephone, a cake under a glass shade, a china sink in the kitchen, a brass gong in the hall to summon the family to meals, and a "cat's whisker" radio.

Another early-20th-century dolls' house belongs to Mrs Lorna Gandolfo, owner of a charming little toy museum in the ancient British town of Sandwich. Her house was made by a master carpenter in 1908, when she was only three years old. It is almost 6 ft (1.8 m) high and so

This English painted-wood dolls' house (RIGHT), *dating from about 1929, is a hand-made model of its owner's new house. It opens front and back and has a central staircase.*

OPPOSITE: *a page from the Lines Brothers 1925–6 catalogue showing four of their dolls' houses, including the thatched-cottage design "made famous" by Queen Mary and, bottom left, a house with a side rather than front opening "so girls can play at houses better".*

Lines' lines are selling lines.

DOLL'S HOUSE DH/1.

Measures 27 inches high, 25 inches wide,
13½ inches deep overall.

A very pretty house with balcony. Finished in
red brick and white enamel. Four rooms with
fireplaces. Nice staircase. Range in Kitchen.

DOLL'S HOUSE DH/3.

Measures 32½ inches high, 31 inches wide,
18 inches deep overall.

A good style Doll's House with four large rooms
and staircase. The interior fittings and curtains
are good.

DOLL'S HOUSE DH/F.

Measures 34 inches wide, 29 inches high,
18½ inches deep overall.

This large house is thoroughly up-to-date in design. It is
finished in pleasing deep colour red brick and tile, with
white rough-cast upper part. The feature is the fixed front
with each end to open, so girls can play at houses better.
No heavy front to swing about.

Interior nicely fitted with fireplaces. Range in Kitchen.
Four large rooms. No staircase.

THE QUEEN'S DOLL'S HOUSE.

Registered Design No. 975508.

26 inches wide, 19 inches high, 16 inches deep.

This Doll's House is an exact reproduction of the
design made famous by Her Majesty the Queen,
who furnished the first model and gave it to the
London Hospital for sale in aid of their funds.
It was bought at the sale for over £300.

58

Father, child, and dachshund in the panelled study of Colles Court (see page 142).

was far too big for her at first. However, when she was older she enjoyed going to Hamleys toy shop in London to buy furniture for it. Most of this furniture was German-made and its import was stopped by World War I. After the war Mrs Gandolfo went back to Hamleys and asked if they still had any pieces of German furniture. They produced a chandelier with one piece missing, which she bought. Many years later, she bought in Wales a doll's house which was completely empty – except for the missing piece of the chandelier – a little miracle which will gladden the heart of any collector.

You can see the chandelier in the drawing room on the second floor of the house, an elegant room with a fine, ornate German metal fireplace, framed portraits (one of Henry VIII), a metal rocking chair, and glass-fronted cupboards containing ornaments. A side table is laid for tea and an ivory chess table, bought in Dieppe between the wars, is set out for a game.

The dining room on the first floor has a fine carpet which was made by Mrs Gandolfo's mother. This room, which boasts an elegant chandelier and landscapes on the walls, is filled with well-made wooden

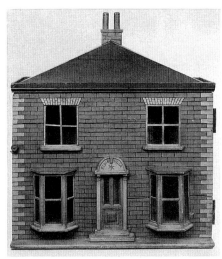

An unpretentious little home-made house (ABOVE) *called Elsie Villa. It has a simulated brick facade and opens to reveal four rooms.*

A small lithographed house of about 1910 (see page 142). Its sunken tower, just visible in the roof, has a pull-string wooden lift.

139

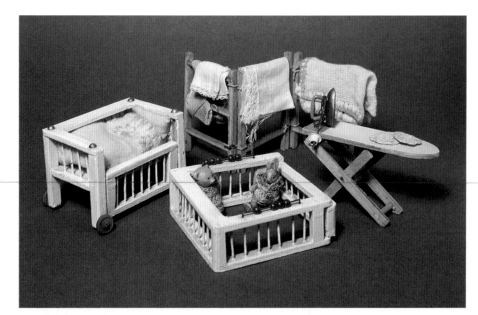

The well-furnished dining room (see page 144) of The Gables *(BELOW) and (RIGHT) Tri-ang furniture from the nursery, including a clothes horse, ironing board, cot, and playpen.*

*A stockbroker Tudor house (*ABOVE*) still bearing the label of its supplier, Hamleys toyshop in London. Probably of the early 1930s, it is the first we have seen to boast an integral garage.*

*Sherwood (*BELOW*), a spectacular house of seventeen rooms in Michal Morse's collection, is dated 1922 over the main door.*

furniture of all kinds – sideboards, a dining table, matching chairs, a writing desk, and corner shelves holding ornaments. On the ground floor is a kitchen, with next to it the housekeeper's sitting room.

Colles Court, c.1920, was left to Faith Eaton by a friend some years ago complete with its wallpapers and furnishings, but without any dolls, which were added later. The house was furnished in the 1920s, but it may have been made a little earlier than this. The plan of the house, which is not a mass-produced model, is unusual in that the service rooms are behind the main rooms. It has a panelled study, a drawing room, a dining room, two bedrooms, two nurseries, and a nanny's room. The back of the house opens in three sections to reveal the bathroom behind the main bedroom, the kitchen behind the study, a day nursery behind the night nursery, and the maid's room behind the nanny's.

The nursery has its original frieze and wallpaper and a white-painted nursery cot. The master bedroom, with its four-poster bed, has furniture by Elgin, a well-known manufacturer of the day. Elgin set up in business at the end of World War I, employing demobilized servicemen and former munitions workers to make furniture to standard patterns supplied by the company. There are printed velvet rugs on the floor and on the bed is a nightdress case of pink silk decorated with appliqué flowers. The drawing room has Tri-ang furniture. The panelled and oak-beamed study has a carved fireplace surround; there is an old wireless on the table, hunting prints on the walls, and ornamental horses on the mantelshelf. Father is about to read a miniature *History of England*.

For the child not lucky enough to be given a hand-made dolls' house, there were plenty of good commercially made houses for sale at affordable prices. Lithographed houses were fashionable in Europe as well as America. The two on page 135, from Mrs Gandolfo's collection, are early 20th century. The balconied house is probably French, the other English, though it is hard to be certain of countries of origin. A lithographed house (page 139) recently sold at auction was described as "English with a pull string wooden lift, the base of the turret missing". It is almost identical in design, even down to the lift and tower, to a dolls' house shown in Jean Latham's book *Dolls' Houses* and described there as a French sea-side villa – and certainly the front door with its wrought-iron grille looks more French than English. But lifts were a feature of the dolls' houses made in Germany by Gottschalk and known to collectors as "Red Roofs".

Commercially made dolls' houses were widely available in England by the beginning of the 20th century. The market leader was the firm of G. & J. Lines. George Lines began as a maker of rocking horses in 1870 and was joined by his brother Joseph in 1880. The first mention of dolls' houses among their wares was in 1898, but it was not until the early years of the 20th century that they became famous for this side of their business. They produced many styles of house, some of which can

OPPOSITE: (TOP RIGHT) *Valerie Ripley's 1932 house, The Gables (see page 144), and* (BOTTOM RIGHT) *the bedroom with its ten-piece Tri-ang Queen Anne suite of furniture.*

and the log book that recorded everything bought or made for the dolls' house.

The bedroom has its original Tri-ang fireplace, although the "coal fire" that fits in it (lit from behind for realistic effect) is home-made. Of special interest is the complete ten-piece Tri-ang Queen Anne bedroom suite (double bed, wardrobe, bow-fronted chest of drawers, dressing mirror, wing-back armchair, stool, occasional table, two ladder-back chairs, and firescreen), originally a boxed set. Some of the same pieces appear in Faith Eaton's Colles Court house and doubtless could once have been found in hundreds of dolls' houses of the period. The carpet came from Hamleys. Inside the wardrobe are period clothes on wooden hangers; on top sits a "leather" suitcase. Over the bed is a framed portrait of the sisters' grandfather as a young man. In the dining room the set of chairs, occasional table, fire screen, and stool are again by Tri-ang, though the canteen of cutlery is by Pit-a-Pat and the dining table and desk are craftsman-made. The charming little home-made box of chocolates is a recent addition. There are some other delightful details in the room – a corkscrew and a metal bottle opener on a drinks' table, a toast rack and a salt shaker on the dining table, and a pair of spectacles and a sepia picture-postcard on the desk.

Faith Eaton's first dolls' house was a 1931 G. & J. Lines house (number 74 in the company's catalogue) with pebble-dash and brick-paper walls and a sundial. It has a porthole window in the gable and another in the garage, which has been turned into a kitchen with a nursery over it. The centre rooms are a bedroom and a lounge; the stairs and bathroom are on the right.

It seems appropriate that a book which began with the grand Nuremberg dolls' houses of the 17th century should end with two equally grand dolls' houses of the 20th century – Titania's Palace, now in Denmark, at Legoland, Copenhagen, and Queen Mary's dolls' house, in England, at Windsor Castle.

Titania's Palace was conceived in 1907 by a British soldier-artist, Sir Nevile Wilkinson. Sir Nevile was sketching a tree near his home in Ireland when his small daughter announced that she had seen a fairy disappearing into the roots of the tree. Sir Nevile chose to believe that the fairy was none other than Titania, queen of all fairies, and offered to build a palace for her and her husband, Oberon. He had undertaken a project which was to fill a large proportion of his remaining lifetime.

He was not without some experience. He had already created the miniature mansion now known as Pembroke Palace (it was "opened" by Queen Alexandra in 1908 and may now be seen at Wilton House in southern England). Pembroke Palace is a large, imposing dolls' house – 6 ft 10½ in (2.1 m) long, 4 ft 1 in (1.25 m) high, and 2 ft 6 in (0.76 m) deep – on three floors. The house as it may be seen today is full of interesting features. The main hall, the dining room, and the double-cube room, although restored, are Sir Nevile's original work. Three of his paintings – portraits of his father-in-law, the 14th Earl of Pembroke, and of his daughter, Gwendoline, and a self-portrait – hang in the double-cube room. All the other paintings in the dolls' house are miniature copies of paintings in Wilton House.

Titania's Palace is far more splendid. It is indeed a palace in miniature, measuring 9 ft (2.75 m) × 7 ft (2.15 m) × 2 ft 3 in (0.7 m), built around a courtyard laid out as a garden and designed to be viewable from all four sides. It is in eight sections, each with a removable front, so that it fits into packing cases when it travels, something it has done frequently to raise money for children's charities. The style of the architecture is varied, with Greek influence showing in the columns, English in the Inigo Jones windows, and Italian in the Palladian frieze and in the Florentine-inspired state apartments.

The eighteen halls and rooms are filled with more than 3,000 small items, some of which are copies of real furniture, paintings, and antiques. There are four state apartments – the Hall of the Fairy Kiss, the chapel, the Hall of the Guilds, and the throne room – all richly decorated with inlay and mosaic, marble and ornaments. Much of the decoration of these rooms was the work of Sir Nevile himself. The elaborate reredos in the chapel took him four years to complete. He invented a sort of pointillistic technique, which gives the impression of mosaic, to paint the palace ceilings.

Most care and time has been lavished on these state apartments. The Hall of the Fairy Kiss is the formal entrance to the palace and it has a beautiful minstrel gallery ornamented with silver and bronze figures, a glass casket containing the Insignia of the Fairy Kiss (the highest order of Fairyland), and miniature statues. On the arches at the side of the room are silver grilles designed to keep the junior fairies from flying into the hall, and portraits of two real-life queens, Mary and Alexandra, each standing by a large dolls' house. As Queen Alexandra opened Pembroke Palace in 1908, it was thought that this might be a picture of it, but Pembroke Palace exterior, a miniature copy of which is in the day nursery of Titania's Palace, is in red brick and does not resemble this imposing-looking building.

The chapel is another fine creation. The reredos contains a miniature copy of a Murillo Madonna; the ceiling is inspired by the Book of Kells. The mosaic windows are made of translucent enamel and the organ can actually be played – with a matchstick. The decorations are typical of the period, similar to those found in dozens of contemporary Anglican churches in England, lavishly decorated in bright, even garish, colours. This love of surface decoration is repeated in the furnishings elsewhere in the palace. A red chest and washstand in the princesses' bedroom closely resemble furniture by William Burges, a famous designer of that time.

The Hall of the Guilds has a coffered ceiling, a black-and-white marble floor, bronze horses, and a miniature mechanical fountain set with diamonds. This room leads to the throne room, whose peacock throne (made out of a brooch believed to have belonged to the Empress

Eugénie) is ornamented with diamonds, rubies, and sapphires. Above the throne is a glass canopy and above that and the windows is a four-inch frieze inspired by one in the Mausoleum of Galla Placidia in Ravenna. In the centre of the room is Titania's pearl-studded royal crown. The names of six writers of fairy tales are perpetuated in the ceiling mosaics.

Fairies were never far from Sir Nevile's thoughts when he built his palace. There are no dolls, so that the palace would always be free for Titania and her court. There is no kitchen, because fairies do not need food. There is, though, and somewhat illogically, a dining room equipped with a glass dinner service but with no knives and forks. Cupboards for the storage of spare wings are provided in the princesses' bedroom. The baths have no drains or taps (because fairies bathe in dewdrops) and none of the doors have handles or knobs (because fairy doors open by themselves).

Titania's Palace was nearing completion when Sir Nevile heard rumours of the existence of Queen Mary's dolls' house. He wrote in his autobiography, "The position was critical, and the fate of twenty years work hung in the balance: for I had promised myself at least a year more to complete the hundred and one details whose absence would be

The Princesses' bedroom in Titania's Palace contains cupboards for the storage of spare fairy wings. The washstand holds a set of Limoges china and monogrammed linen hangs from a silver towel rack.

noticed when Titania's Palace faced the footlights. But delay meant being overtaken and overshadowed by the splendid creation of Sir Edwin Lutyens and his thousand helpers''. In fact, Titania's Palace was exhibited, unfinished, at an exhibition in 1922, and "opened" by Queen Mary.

The idea of presenting Queen Mary with a dolls' house had been conceived in 1920 as a token of goodwill towards her and as a means of raising money for the many charities in which she was interested. The house was first shown in public at the British Empire Exhibition at Wembley in 1924, it travelled extensively in the 1920s and it still raises funds from its home in Windsor Castle.

Queen Mary's dolls' house has been described as being "so perfect as to seem incredible". Just as the Duchess Dorothea's rooms at Arnstadt show court life of the 18th century, Queen Mary's mansion depicts a court residence of the 20th century. It is a unique record of life in a very wealthy household.

It is a model rather than a dolls' house, because it has never been played with and every detail, down to the smallest item, is meticulously executed. Nearly everything in it was especially commissioned, unlike Titania's Palace, in which some of the items were second-hand.

The Hall of the Fairy Kiss, the formal entrance hall of Titania's Palace.

Looking at the rooms, it is hard to realize that we are not looking at a full-size house, but the dolls'-house scale of one-twelfth real size always poses problems for designers, because, as all dolls'-house owners know, materials behave in different ways when used on a small scale. Fabrics, for example, fall too stiffly. Paper cannot be reduced to a thinner size, and substitutes often have to be found. "The door locks, throughout the house", wrote Sir Clifford Musgrave "are marvels of ingenuity. For a full size mansion of this character locks with eight levers would have been used, but such levers to proper scale would only have been of paper thickness, so three levers only are used, which is the normal number for an ordinary house. They all work with perfect smoothness and efficiency. The only difficulty is for a human being to turn the tiny keys."

The house was very up-to-date for its time, with electric light, piped hot and cold water, electric vacuum cleaners, irons, and other labour-saving devices. Many of them, like the coal-burning range in the kitchen, are now period pieces, and the provision of "pneumonia packets" in the nursery suite reminds us of how difficult it was to nurse sick children in pre-antibiotic days.

The building, designed by Sir Edwin Lutyens, took four years to complete. It looks a little like Buckingham Palace from one side; it is made of wood painted to resemble Portland stone and stands on a base which contains storage space for dolls – though there are no dolls in the house. The base also contains workrooms, cellars, machinery, and a well-fitted garage with six limousines like those used by the queen in her daily life.

That great gardener Gertrude Jekyll planned the garden, which is contained in a drawer, the trees lying flat when the drawer is closed, as do the gate and the balustrade. Lawns are made of green velvet, flower beds are planted with irises, roses, lilies, marigolds, and other summer flowers, all fashioned in different metals. Magnolia plants are trained against the masonry; climbing roses trail over the niches of the back wall and there are charming details such as a fairy-ring of toadstools growing on a path, snails, butterflies, birds in trees, and even eggs in a thrush's nest.

Inside, the most important room on the west front is the walnut-panelled library, its cabinets holding over seven hundred prints, water-colours, and drawings by famous artists of the day and two hundred leather-bound books by well-known authors, written in their own handwriting – Hilaire Belloc, Walter de la Mare, Thomas Hardy, and Rudyard Kipling among them. H. G. Wells, George Bernard Shaw, and John Masefield declined to take part in the game. On a chest is a group of fourteen red despatch boxes from government departments and the king's desk is littered with books, photographs, a bottle of ink, a letter opener, a reading lamp, a cheque book, and cigarettes.

Over the library is the king's bedroom, a magnificent room with a painted ceiling, its wall panels painted in Chinese style. Above the

THE 20TH CENTURY

fireplace is Ambrose McEvoy's portrait of Princess Mary, while the bed resembles a pink silk Indian temple, ornamented with ostrich feathers. Off the king's bedroom is the king's wardrobe, in which white cupboards hold minute uniforms. On the opposite side is the king's bathroom, which has a white marble floor, a green marble bath, and silver taps. The doll king, had there been one, could have lain in his bath and gazed at the vaulted ceiling decorated with scenes of the expulsion from paradise.

The queen's bedroom has a similarly elaborate canopied four-poster bed hung with damask silk, pale blue-grey silk walls, a fine dressing table draped with pleated silk, a walnut writing table with tiny handles to the drawers, a gilt day bed, and a handsome wardrobe with working lock and key. A painting of the queen's mother, the Duchess of Teck, hangs over the 18th-century-style chimney piece and there is a diamond-framed mirror on the dressing table.

The queen's bathroom, which leads off the bedroom, has a mother-of-pearl floor and an alabaster bath with silver taps. Water

The imposing entrance hall of Queen Mary's dolls' house. The whole outer shell of the house can be raised so that the interior may be viewed from all four sides.

151

circulates slowly in miniature pipes, but as Percy Macquoid wrote, lyrically: "It is one of the prettiest sights in the world to·see the bath tub filled with water, the drops swelling slowly from the taps until the whole room is reflected in them, with indescribable minute beauty; and the reflection of the mother-of-pearl and of the paintings on the ceiling, given added colour to the natural iridescence of these globes of water". Queen Mary was given a ceiling painting of mermaids bathing in a pool.

Her sitting room is furnished with amber and jade ornaments, a lovely cream and gold lacquer cabinet, and a handwoven copy of a Chinese rug of the Chien-Lung period. The glass cabinets are filled with tiny articles of Chinese porcelain and jade, all of which must have been to her real Majesty's taste.

Above the queen's bedroom is the day nursery, its walls decorated with nursery-rhyme murals and furnished with a dolls' room, a train set, and a gramophone that plays "God Save the King". A toy theatre, lit by electric light, is set for a performance of *Peter Pan*. Also on the nursery floor is the Princess Royal's room, with a mahogany four-poster bed; under the mattress is a real pea, grown to the correct scale, a reference to the fairy tale of the princess and the pea. The night nursery contains a tiny cradle of polished apple-wood inlaid and bound with silver, the inside lined with ivory.

The dining room is another little masterpiece. Panelled in early-

OPPOSITE: *the King's bedroom in Queen Mary's dolls' house, with its 18th-century state bed, tasseled chandelier, and portrait of Queen Mary over the fireplace.*

White filigree metal furniture (BELOW) *made in the 1920s by the Diessen firm of Schweitzer, which was established in 1796.*

18th-century style, it has a painted ceiling depicting figures in landscapes. The grey walls are decorated with carved fruit and flowers in limewood picked out in gold. The dining table can be extended or closed and is laid with cloth bearing the royal monogram and set with silver tableware, glass, silver candelabra, and fruit on porcelain dishes. Over the fireplace is a portrait of the Prince of Wales (later King Edward VIII) in the hunting field, painted by Sir Alfred Munnings, who also painted the animal pictures on either side of the fireplace.

The working rooms are no less interesting than the state rooms. Off the dining room is the butler's pantry, equipped with glass decanters, goblets, porcelain and silver coffee pots, and even a small tin

A set of 1920s German rococo furniture (ABOVE RIGHT) – *a grandfather clock, two chairs, a commode, and a sideboard.*

Household items from The Gables (RIGHT) – *the stove is by Taylor & Barrett, the pans by Britains. The mangle, vacuum cleaner, and sewing machine are German.*

of Colman's mustard. Above the pantry is the strong room, where the crown jewels in tiny replica are protected by a steel grille, while other jewels are kept in a safe with a working combination lock.

The linen room contains a stock of hand-woven Irish linen. The wine cellar is stocked with bottles of real 1922 vintage wines, with beer and whisky in bottles and casks, and with a selection of brandies and other liqueurs and soft drinks. The kitchen has tiled walls, a wood-block floor with a strip of slate set in front of the Crittall cooking range, and a hot cupboard and pastry oven along one wall. The cat and the mouse in a trap lend a little life to an otherwise austere setting. In the scullery are the deep lead-lined sinks into which real hot water can run from outsize taps, which are about the only out-of-scale items in the whole house.

MINIATURES

Fortunately for collectors, it is still possible to buy pieces of early-20th-century dolls'-house furniture from time to time.

Factories all over the world produced the furniture commercially and in great quantity. Germany was exporting furniture up to and after World War I, in tried and tested designs in traditional metal and wood and in new, experimental materials such as celluloid. The long-established firm of Schweitzer at Diessen specialized in filigree metal furniture and is still in production today. Other German firms continued to make wooden pieces similar in shape to the lithographed paper-on-wood furniture of the previous century. However, they were sufficiently aware of the changing taste of their young clients to produce at the same time up-to-date household equipment such as miniature vacuum cleaners, sewing machines, and mangles. The firm of Märklin,

A New Testament (LEFT) *and an opal casket* (RIGHT) *from Titania's Palace.*

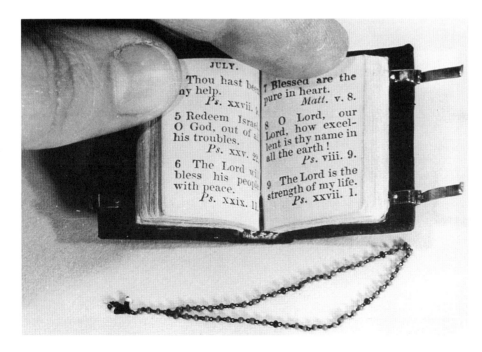

founded in the previous century, continued to manufacture a large range of dolls'-house furniture in metal and wood until the the 1930s.

In Britain, Elgin and Tri-ang made attractive wooden furniture in Queen Anne, Chippendale, Empire, or Adam style (all popular styles in suburban houses of the time), upholstered in friendly chintzes. Tri-ang and Elgin furniture looks much alike and, as Constance Eileen King points out in *The Collector's History of Dolls' Houses*, some of the furniture sold by Tri-ang may have been manufactured by smaller firms, then packed and marketed by Tri-ang.

Pit-a-Pat was another English firm producing high-quality wooden furniture and dolls'-house oddments in the early 20th century. Taylor & Barratt were successful with the metal gas fires and gas stoves which are frequently seen in dolls' houses of this period. William Britain made a range of dolls'-house equipment which included heavy kitchen saucepans with lids.

An interesting range of metal furniture sometimes found in 1930 dolls' houses was called Dolly Varden and was made by Meccano in its Dinky Toy range. Very rare now, these were small – a chair was only

A suite of furniture by Elgin, from Colles Court dolls' house.

1½ in (4 cm) high – and collapsible cardboard houses could be bought separately to contain them.

American manufacturers were also active in the dolls'-house furnishing field and were exporting their goods all over the world. Tootsie Toy's brightly coloured metal furniture was a leader in the American market for several years and can still be seen in some English dolls' houses. The range included furniture for every room in the house.

The firm of R. Bliss had started making miniature furniture in the 1890s, though it was not intended to fit into their dolls' houses, which were smaller in scale than the furniture. The sturdily made wooden pieces were decorated with pictures in bright colours.

Alongside this commercial activity were craftsman-made pieces, exemplified by the beautiful objects in Titania's Palace and Queen Mary's dolls' house. This long tradition of good craftsmanship continues to this day, for discerning dolls'-house collectors can buy not only mass-produced plastic items – many of which are excellently designed – but the lovingly made little pieces which are obtainable from small craft shops and studios all over the world.

OVERLEAF
A cello, a whatnot, a chair, and a jardinière from Titania's Palace.

Brightly decorated furniture, with scenes of children at play, made by the firm of Rufus Bliss, which began manufacture in the 1890s.

BIBLIOGRAPHY

Baker, Roger, *Dolls and Dolls' Houses*, Orbis, London, 1973

Cook, Dorothy, *Dolls' Houses on the Printed Page*, London, 1966

Eveleigh, David, *Firegrates and Kitchen Ranges*, Shire Publications, Aylesbury, 1983

Fearn, Jacqueline, *Domestic Bygones*, Shire Publications, Aylesbury, 1977

Flick, Pauline, *The Dolls' House Book*, William Collins, London, 1973

Greene, Vivien, *English Dolls' Houses of the 18th and 19th Centuries*, B. T. Batsford Ltd, London, 1955 (reissued 1979)

—— *Family Dolls' Houses*, G. Bell & Sons, London, 1973

Gröber, Karl, *Children's Toys of Bygone Days*, B. T. Batsford Ltd, London, 1928

Jackson, Mrs F. Nevill, *Toys of Other Days*, Country Life, George Newnes, London, and Charles Scribner's Sons, New York, 1908

Jacobs, Flora Gill, *Dolls' Houses in America*, Charles Scribner's Sons, New York, 1974

—— *A History of Dolls' Houses,* Charles Scribner's Sons, New York, 1953, and Cassell, London, 1954

—— *Victorian Dolls' Houses*, Washington Dolls' House and Toy Museum, Washington, D.C., 1978

A World of Dolls' Houses, Rand McNally & Co., Chicago, 1965

King, Constance Eileen, *The Collector's History of Dolls' Houses*, Robert Hale Ltd, London, 1983

—— *Dolls and Dolls' Houses*, Hamlyn, London, 1977

Latham, Jean, *Dolls' Houses,* A. & C. Black, London, 1969

Toller, Jane, *Miniature Furniture in Great Britain and the United States*, G. Bell & Sons, London, 1966

Whitton, Blair (ed), *Bliss Toys and Doll Houses*, Dover Publications Inc., New York

Wilckens, Leoni von, *The Dolls' House,* Bell & Hyman, London, 1980

—— *Mansions in Miniature*, Viking, London

INDEX

Figures in *italics* refer to captions to illustrations

Albrecht, Duke of Bavaria 9–10
Alexandra, Queen 146, 147
Alnwick Castle 102
Amstel, Sara Ploos Van, houses of
44–9, *78, 79,* 80
Amsterdam
Rijksmuseum 33, 34, 41, 49
Andrew, Barbara, house of 84
angel beds 58–60
Angus, Bridget 104
Anne, Princess (later Queen) 36,
38
Appel, Jacob 33
Arnstadt Castle Museum 44
Audley End 97–100, 120, *123,* 124
Augusta Dorothea, Duchess,
house of 43–4

Basel
Historisches Museum 24, 97
Baumann, Dorothea 94
Baumler house *19,* 20–21
Bel Air house 115, *116*
Bennett, Emma 109
Bergen
Vestlandkse
Kunstindustrimuseum 75
Berlin
Castle Museum 24
Bidden house 101
Biedermeier furniture 113,
120–21
Blaauw house 46–9, *80*
Blackett house 64–6
Bliss, Rufus 115, 130–32, 157
Brett house 111–13
Britain, William *154,* 156
Brown, George C. 114
Bryant, Mrs, house of 105–6
Buttener 49

Cane End house 69, *71,* 109
Carlsro house 92
Castle Howard 69
Cedars, the 101
Chamberlain house 114, *115*
Charlotte, Queen 69
Chicago
Museum of Science and
Industry 133
China, ancient 7
Chippendale, Thomas 56–7, 69
Claremont House 104–5, *106*
Clarétie, Leo 35, 72
Clayton, David 80
Colles Court *138,* 142, *142,* 146,
156
Constable, Zandra 130
Contented Cot 109–10
Converse 115–16, 132
Copenhagen
Dansk Folkemuseum 72, 92
Corinth, toys from 7
Cottrell, G. W. 116
Court, Petronella de la, house
29–33
Crete, toys from 7
Currie family 106

Denver
Rosenberg collection 28–9, 53,
54
Devonshire Villas 133–6
Dibb family 115
Diessen furniture 104, 120, *153,*
155
Dimple Villa 118
Dingley Hall 106
Dinky Toys 156–7
dolls 9, 10, 17–20, 24, 28, 29, 33,
34, 35, 36, 37, 43–4, 49, 52, 75,
86, 91–2, 100, 108, 109, 128, 136
in Blackett house 65, 66
in Hammond House 104
in Nostell Priory 57, 58
in Uppark 60–61
Dolly Varden furniture 156–7
doofpots 52, *80*
Dordrecht
Simon van Gijn museum 52, *53,*
55
Dunois, Petronella, house 34–5, 42

Eaton, Faith 108–10, 129–30, 142,
146
Egypt, ancient 7
Elgin 142, 156
Elsie Villa *139*
English Toy Company 118
Eugénie, Empress 148

Faurholt, Estrid 92
Fetherstonhaugh, Harry 61
Fetherstonhaugh, Sir Matthew 58
filigree furniture 120, *125, 153,*
155
Flick, Pauline, quoted 97–100
Flierden family 66–8
folding houses *4,* 116–18, 132
food 126
foot warmers 35
Francis, Field and Francis 125
Frankfurt
Stadtisches Historisches
Museum 44
Frederick VIII, king of Denmark
94
Frederick, Prince of Wales 53
Fremont
Rutherford B. Hayes library
114
fretwork furniture 124, *126*
Friedman, Anna, house 94–5, *97*

Gables, The *140, 142,* 144–6, *154*
Gandolfo, Lorna 130, *135,*
136–42, *145*
Gontard house 44
Gothic house *101,* 102
Gottschalk 142
"Grandmother's dolls' house" 92
Greece, ancient 7
Greene, Vivien 68, 81, 100, 101,
102, 108, 109, 111, *118*
quoted 56, 105
houses in collection of 56, 69,
100–02

Grimston Garth 102
Gröber, Karl 8, 43
Groenendijk, Peter van 34
Gustavus Adolphus II, king of
Sweden 24

Haarlem
Frans Hals museum 49
Hacker, Christian 84
Hagen house 72
Hague, The
Gemeente Museum 44, 80, 84,
89
Hainhofer, Philip 24
Hallberg house *95*
Hall, Henry 109
Hamilton, Emma 61
Hamleys 139, *141,* 146
Hammond house 104, *106,* 124
Hartley Hall 110, *111*
hasteners 69
Hayes house 114
Helsinki
Museovirasto 94, *95,* 128
Henry II, king of France 9
Henry IV, king of France 9
Hersbyholm Manor 128
Heslington family 69
Hinderloopen furniture 87
Holme, C. G. 24
Homans family 76
Hooch, Peter de 33
Jackson, Mrs F. Nevill 9
quoted 20, 24, 40, 180
Jacobs, Flora Gill
collection of 113
quoted 36, 97, 113
James, Edward 26, 28
James, Evelyn 28
Japanese house and furniture
129–30, *145*
Jekyll, Gertrude 150

Kansas City
W. R. Nelson Gallery of Art 7
Kelterborn, Ludwig Adam 97
Kihlberg, Emelie, house *91,* 92
King, Constance Eileen 156
quoted 120–21
King's Lynn House 66–8, *71*
Kits Coty house *6,* 144
Koferlin, Anna, house of 13
Kress house 17–20

Latham, Jean 142
laundry rooms 33
Legoland 92
Lethioullier, Sarah 58, 61
lignum-vitae ware 39, 40, 77, 78
Lines, G. & J. *6, 111,* 142–4, 146
Lines Brothers *136,* 144
see also Tri-ang
Loebe, Samuel 133–4
Lojander family 128–9
London
Bethnal Green Museum of
Childhood 23, 36, 40, *41,* 64,
103, 105, 106, *108, 110,* 133

British Museum 7
Museum of London 65, 97
Loofs, Adam 40
Louis, Dauphin (later Louis XIII)
9
Lutyens, Sir Edwin 149, 150

Maas, Mrs *73*
McLoughlin folding house *4,* 116
Macquoid, Percy
quoted 153
Manchester
Wythenshaw collection 110–11
Marie Antoinette 72
Märklin 155–6
Mary, Princess (later Queen) 40,
97, 147, 149, 151
see also Queen Mary's dolls'
house
Meket-Re 7
Melos, toys from 7
Miles, Amy 106
Miss Miles' House 106–7
Mon Plaisir 43–4, *46,* 53
Moore, Colleen, house of 133
Moreland, George 56
Morley, Lord 101
Morse, Michal *141*
Mrs Bryant's Pleasure 105–6
Munich
Bayerisches Nationalmuseum
24
Duke Albrecht's museum 24
Stadtmuseum *83,* 84
Munnings, Sir Alfred 154–5
Musgrave, Sir Clifford
quoted 150

National Trust, The 101, 103
New York
City Museum 111, 113, 132
Metropolitan Museum of Art 7
Strong Museum 53, 84, 86
Van Cortlandt Museum 76
Nostell Priory house 56–8, *60, 61,*
77
Nuremberg
furniture from 120
Germanisches Nationalmuseum
12, 13, 17, 20, 23, 29, 82
and toy industry 8, 80, 84
Spielzeugmuseum *82,* 118, 127

Oortman, Petronella, house *30,*
32, 33, 41–2
Orly furniture 120, *123*
Osterburg Castle 8

Paine, James 56
Paris
Musée des Arts Décoratifs 90,
127
Musée des Arts et Traditions
Populaires 90
Pembroke Palace 146–7
pewter miniatures 40, 77, *123*
Philip, Duke of Pomerania *8,* 24
Piemont, Nicolaas 33

Pit-a-Pat 144, 146, 156
Plaats, David Van Der 44
Portobello Road house 69
Puebla, house from 114

Queen Mary's dolls' house 149–55

Ramsay Grano 94
"Red Roofs" 142
Ripley, Valerie *142*, 144–6
Romney, George 61
Rosenberg, Dr 28–9, 53
Rotunda, the 56, 69, 100
Russell, Mrs 116
Russian dolls' houses 132, *145*
Ruyter, Margaretha de 34

Sadeler, Jan 12
St Faith's Vicarage 101
Salem
   Essex Institute 113
Saltram House 101
Sandtner, Jacob 10
Schneegas 121
Schoenhut 115, *130*, 132
Schwartz 84
Schweitzer *153*, 155

"Scroll Saw" designs 124
Sharp, Ann, house 36–40
Sharp, John 36
shaving mirrors 78
Shelton Taylor house 113
Sherwood *141*
silver miniatures 9, 10, 30, 33, 37,
   39, 40, 41, 42, 49, 77, 80, 84, 86,
   113, 114
Sodra Lindved castle 36
Somer, Bernardus 34
Sotheby's 87, 92, 110, *130*
Stack House 100, *102*
Stettheimer house 132–3
Stevens, J. and S., Company
   125–6
Stockholm
   Nordiska Museet 35, 75, 91, 128
Strangers' Hall house 68–9, *71*
Strasbourg
   Musée de l'Oeuvre de Notre
      Dame 24
Stroner house 13–7

Tarquinia Museum 7
Tate, Mrs Walter 64
Tate house 64, *65*

Taylor & Barrett 144, *154*, 156
Three Sisters house 94
Thuringian ware 104, 120
Tiffany family 113
Titania's Palace *4*, 146–9, *154*, *158*
Tootsie Toy 144, 157
Tradescant, John 37
travelling house 56, *57*
Tri-ang 142, 144, 146, 156
Tunbridge ware 77, 78

Uppark house 58–61, *63*, *64*, 77
Uppsala, house at 24
Utrecht
   Centraal Museum 29

Van Cortlandt house 76
Vanbrugh, Sir John 69
Vanderstregen family 69
Victoria, Queen 69, 97
Vienna
   Museum Angewandte Kunste 24
Villa Olga 92–3, *95*

Waarenburg, Christiaan 33, 41
Wallington Hall, houses in 103–5,
   106

Walterhausen furniture 91, 95,
   104, 120, *124*
Warren house 113–14, *116*
Washington
   Dolls' House and Toy Museum
      113, 114–15, 126
   Smithsonian Institute 114
washstands 78
Wedgwood 124
Welch, Denton 125
West Dean house 26–8, 40–41,
   42
Whiteway 100–01
Wilcken, Leoni von 28
Wilkinson, Sir Nevile 133, 146,
   147, 148–9
Wilton House 146, 147
Windsor Castle 149
Winn, Sir Rowland 56
Wit, Jacob de 49

Yarburgh house 69
Yoakley Lodge 109
York
   Castle Museum 69

Zintl's house 84, *86*

ACKNOWLEDGEMENTS

I would like to thank the following people whose generous help has enabled me to write this book : Faith Eaton, who kindly allowed me to study her books and to use photographs of the dolls' houses in her collection; Mrs Graham Greene, who allowed me access to the Rotunda, Oxford; Nick Nicholson, of Hawkley Studios, who took a great many of the photographs, often in difficult circumstances; and the owners of some of the dolls' houses featured – Captain and Mrs Bulwer Long, Mrs Maas, Mrs Barbara Andrew, Mrs Lorna Gandolfo (The Precinct Toy Collection, Sandwich), Michal Morse (The Dolls' House, Covent Garden), Valerie Ripley, and Mrs Zandra Constable.

I owe especial thanks to Mrs Flora Gill Jacobs, to whom I am indebted for my information on American dolls' houses.

PICTURE CREDITS

Pages 2, 148, 149, 155, 158 Legoland; 25 © Historisches Museum, Basel, photo M. Babey; 31, 32, 34 © Rijksmuseum, Amsterdam; 35, 74, 75, 91, 128 (right, top and bottom) Nordiska Museet, Stockholm; 47 Arnstadt Museum; 48, 80 © Frans Hals Museum, Haaglemi, photo Tom Haartsen; 51, 78, 88-9 Haags Gemeentemuseum; 54 Denver Art Museum, Denver, Colorado; 68 © King's Lynn Social History Museum; 77 (top), 87 (right), 111 (bottom right), 112, 120, 121, 122 (bottom), 123 (bottom), 124, 136, 139 Sotheby's; 86, 87 (left) © Bayerisches National Museum, Munich; 95, 96, 129 National Museum of Finland, Helsinki; 108, 110, 153 Bridgeman Art Library; 115 Courtesy of the Wenham Museum, Wenham, MA. Photo by Mark Sexton; 116, 130 Washington Dolls' House and Toy Museum; 117 Courtesy of the Essex Institute, Salem, MA; 125 Idion Verlag Munchen, 1979, in *Schönes Spielzeug*; 127 (left), 154 (top) Ineichen, Zürich; 127 (right) Collection du Musée des Arts Décoratifs, Paris, photo Laurent Sully-Jaulmes; 128 (left) Spielzergmuseum, Nuremberg; 137 Phillips; 141 (bottom) Michal Morse; 151, 152 Reproduced by gracious permission of Her Majesty the Queen. Photographs not otherwise credited above are by Hawkley Studio.